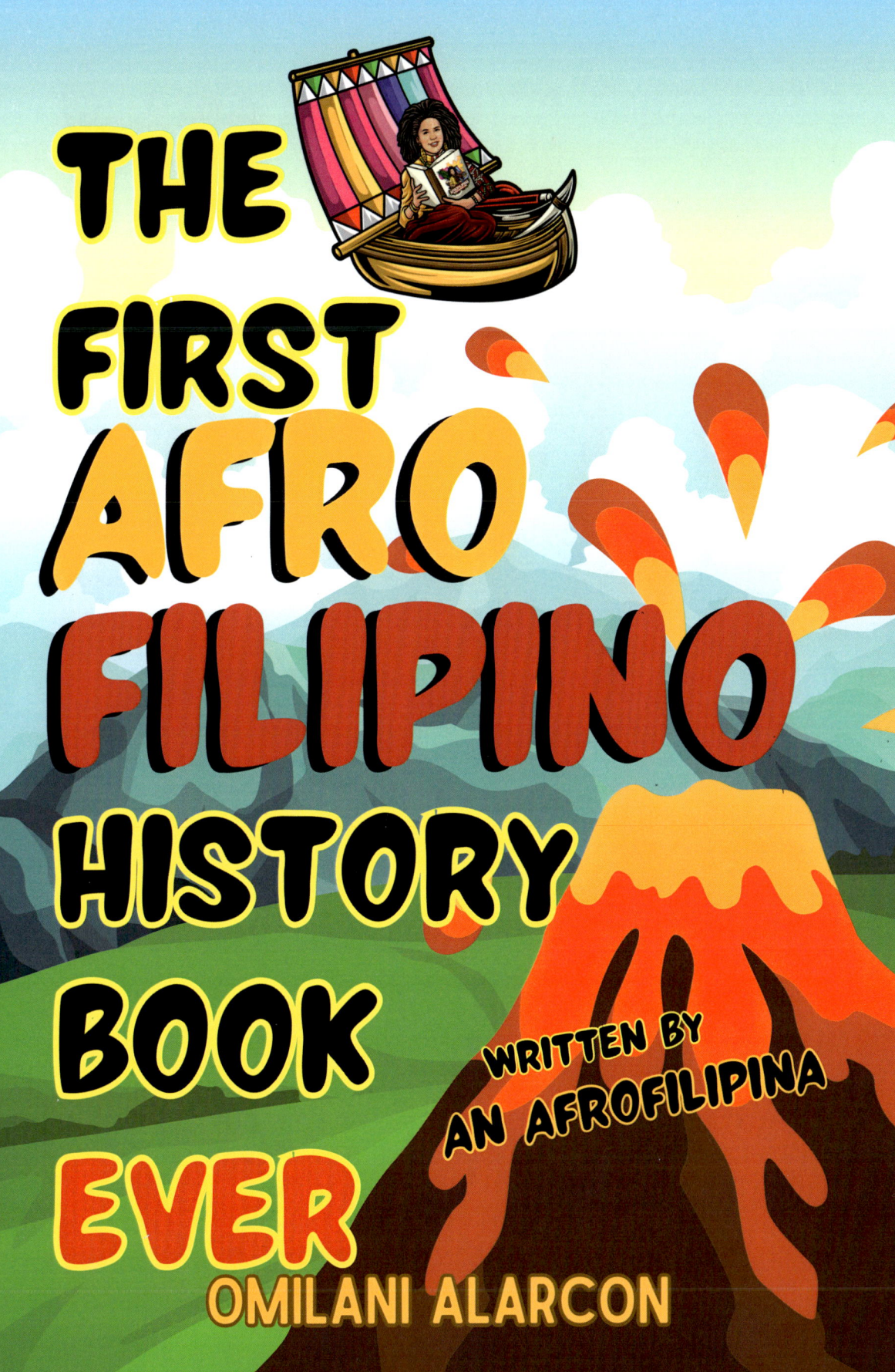

DISCLAIMER

This book is not for the faint at heart. It is a true account of the experience of the AfroFilipino diaspora worldwide through the lens of an afrofilipina. This book aims to share the untold/rejected history that has been hidden, swept under the rug, and ignored. This book is decolonial and not written in dense academic language because it is intended to be accessible to anyone who would like to read and know more. I have never seen any books on what it is like being Black and Filipino written by a black filipino - or by anybody for that matter (that doesn't mean they don't exist. I just havent seen any). That is why i have written this book - so little girls and boys who are like me will not have the same struggles I had growing up without any representation.

afrofilipino history is also an important part of filipino history and of our journey in the diaspora.

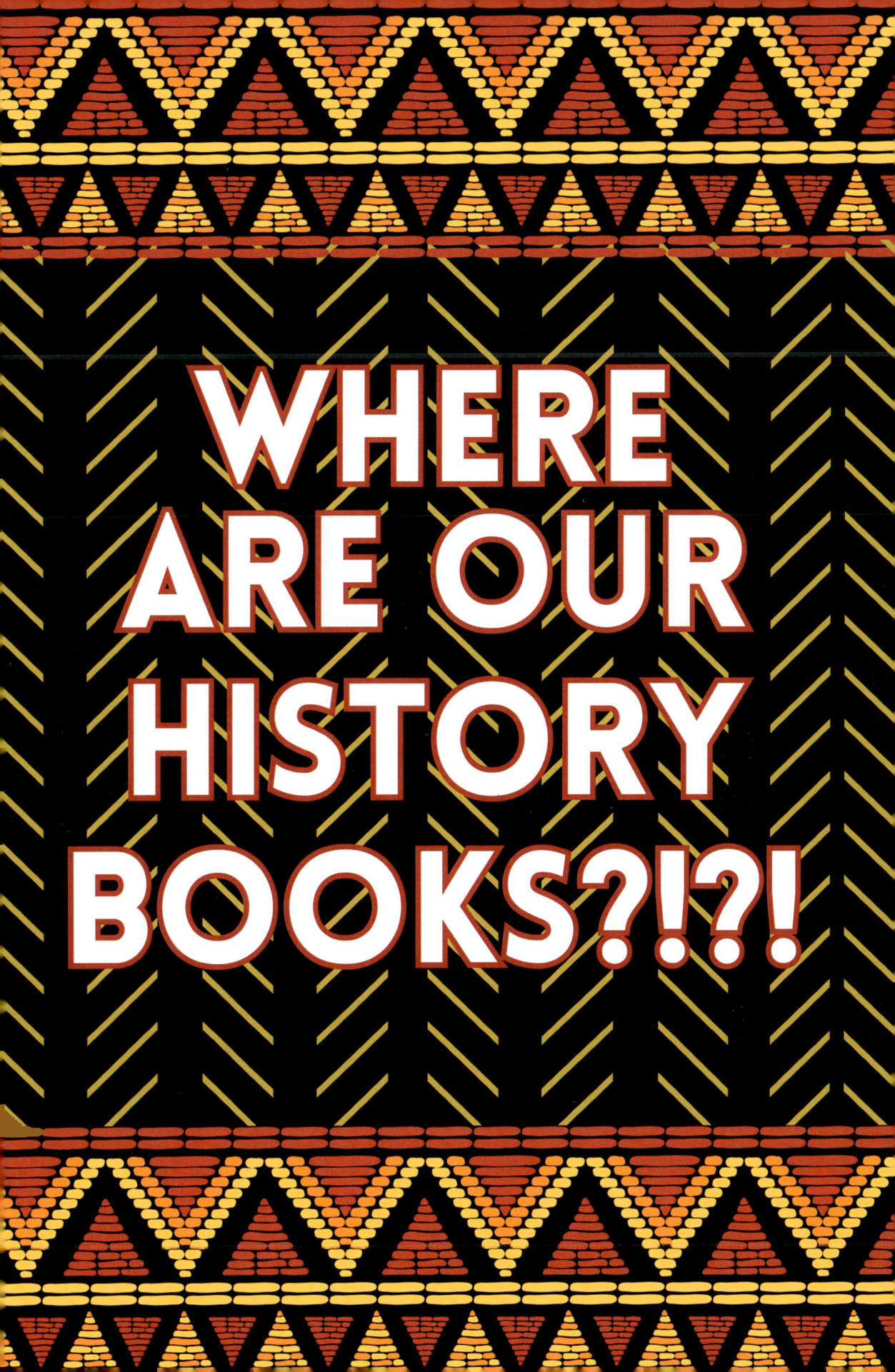

> *Believe it or not i can actually draw*
> — Jean Michel Basquiat

A CONSCIOUS ACADEMIC?
OMILANI ALARCON

The crux of being an academic and an activist is that it is like a tortuous pendulum that tilts back and forth between the elitist stratification that produces "Masters" and the struggle to remain connected to community after years of being in an environment so separate and so different from the places we call home. We often had debates about this subject as I was matriculating through degrees at some of the world's top institutions of higher learning. Sitting in ornate classrooms at a university with a 10 billion dollar endowment, my colleagues and I would ponder about academia and community along with our place in it. With our eyes set on the horizon of a fresh Ivy League degree - in Africana Studies nonetheless, we would ask, **"Do you think it is possible to be conscious and an academic?"**

In our comfortable dorm rooms that reeked of old money and entitled bigotry, we would go back and forth until the wee hours of the morning discussing how, with more resources, we would be better assets to our community. The deeper I got into academia (and I was excellent at it), the more academia began to turn my stomach.

Post graduation, my colleagues separated into groups that either scrambled for job placements or decided to *play the game* in hopes of making tenure. I was not cut out for either of those paths. I was just too rebellious and way too free.

Yet, independence has its challenges. It did not solve the question of how I would be able to take the knowledge I have acquired through the years and make it accessible to the people.

I believed music would be the ideal path for me, given how transformative and influential it can be, music, film and fashion became my ways of sharing knowledge and culture with the world. When not touring, I participated in numerous community-based activist projects, leveraging my skills and expertise to effect change. This fusion of academics and community engagement proved fulfilling, and I was content with the impact I was making... *At least I thought I was.*

After gaining recognition as an artist, I noticed a shift in how people perceived me. I felt that I was no longer taken seriously as an intellectual. Honors cords and summa cum laude do not matter when you are young, Black, and an eccentric, **full-figured** woman.

I was falling deep into a well of confusion and frustration, trapped between worlds that did not *see* each other. So I decided to seek answers from within to define my purpose. I came to realize that I am *more* than just the **work** I do. I am a full being not defined by categories. I am the equator **and** the prime meridian tilting on an axis of Africa and the blue Pacific seas. These identities are connected. We are not just *phenotype* and migration theories. **Our souls remember each other**.

Before I *consciousness* was on the horizon, I was born a *spiritual being*. A granddaughter of Mindanao. In my blood lies the secrets of the *T'nalak* **dreamweavers** and they called me home. AfroFilipina History & Culture is a spiritual journey and a dedication to **all** of you.

RUNNING AWAY FROM THE GROUND

Can you run away from the ground? I sure tried, because for years I let people convince me I was not Filipino. I loathed my Filipino roots and ran as far as I could from them, until I understood *Filipino* beyond the governmental meaning. If I detach the colonizer's definitions and strings and if I recall that my Ancestors are buried by those seas and in those mountains - that we survived tsunamis and earthquakes - rebellions and invasions - That I cannot drain the blood that runs through my veins just because my *being* **offends** people.

Yet, I am stubborn and for years I ran away from the ground where my roots were anchored. Then suddenly odd things started happening. Dreams and coincidences forced me to put my feet on the ground and to stop running away.

The *coincidences* were so exact and so bizarre that they were undeniable. Those dreams led me to find my long lost family from the Philippines and to grow AfroFilipina from 35 followers to the channel and the projects that are completed today.

Through my Ancestors, I realized that my purpose in life has nothing to do with the questions limited to *conscious academia*. I was born to follow the path that was carved in the dirt before me, lest I become like a tree with no roots.

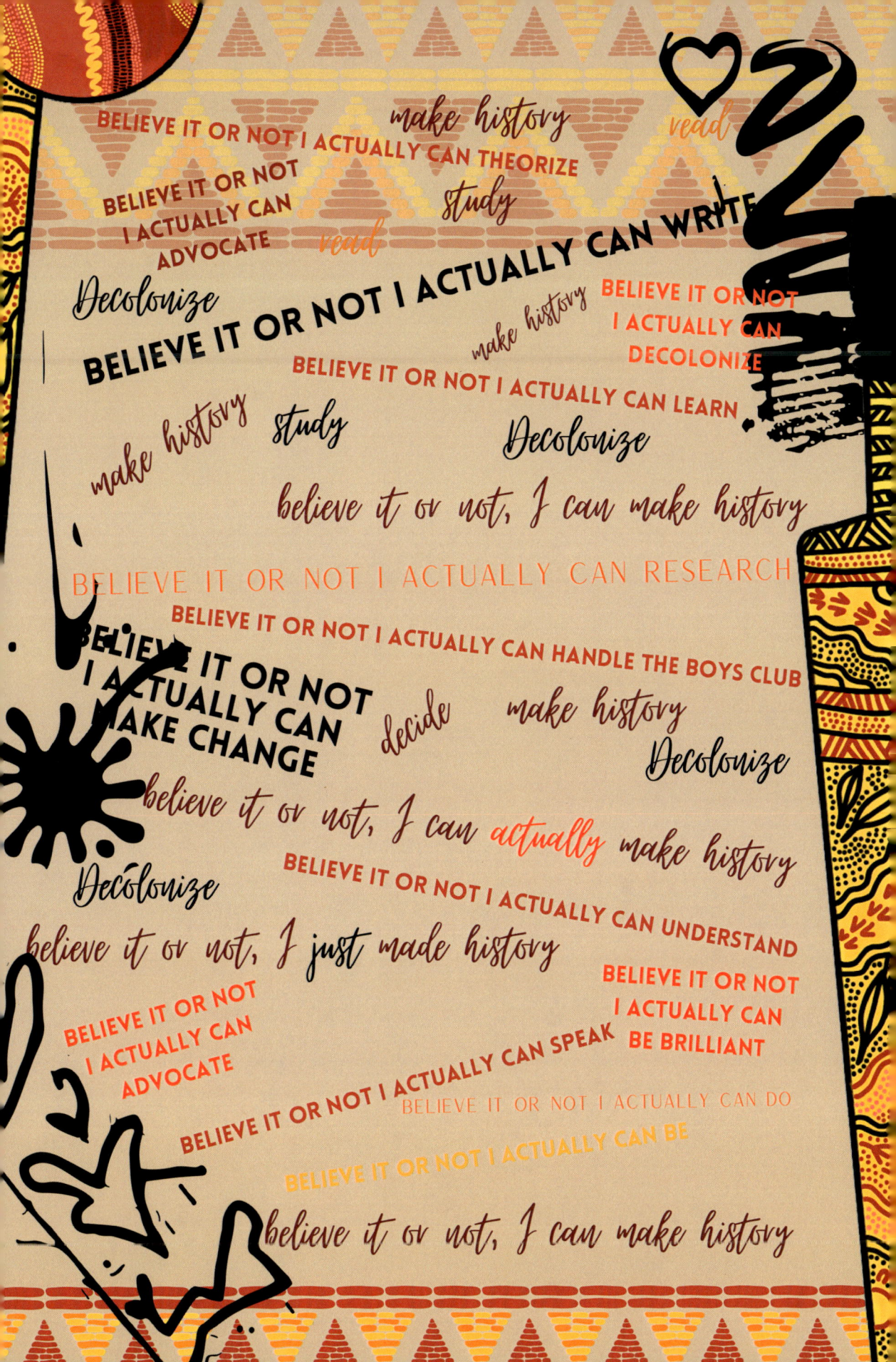

DEDICATION

When i was growing up, Filipino Black History books were not in existance. As a matter of fact, at the time of writing this book, to my knowledge there are NO Black History books dedicated solely to the history, culture and experience of BLACK, DARK SKINNED, CURLY HAIRED, UNIQUE, FULL FIGURED, AFRO HAIRED, AFRICAN LOOKING FILIPINOS - WHO GLISTEN IN THE SUN AND LEARNED TO LOVE THEIR FLAT NOSES.

We be the Black peole of the FILIPINO diaspora and we do not fit into the mainstream. This book is to uplift OUR voices, OUR history, and to look in the face of our connection between the dark-skinned indigenous communities and the African diaspora because we encounter many of the same challenges in this world, based on our phenotype and economic disadvantages and journeys that have come at the hands of history.

It is the most amazing honor to be a Black Latinegra woman academic and a proud AFROFILIPINA. This is for ALL of us and it is just the beginning. We need to keep telling OUR stories in OUR voices.

This is OUR book - dedicated to the Filipino and Black dispora and to all of the Halo-Halo people trying to understand where they fit in this Black and White world. Embrace all of your beautiful colors and live out loud!!!

Sincerely,

AfroFilipina

Omilani Alarcon - Founder AfroFilipina®

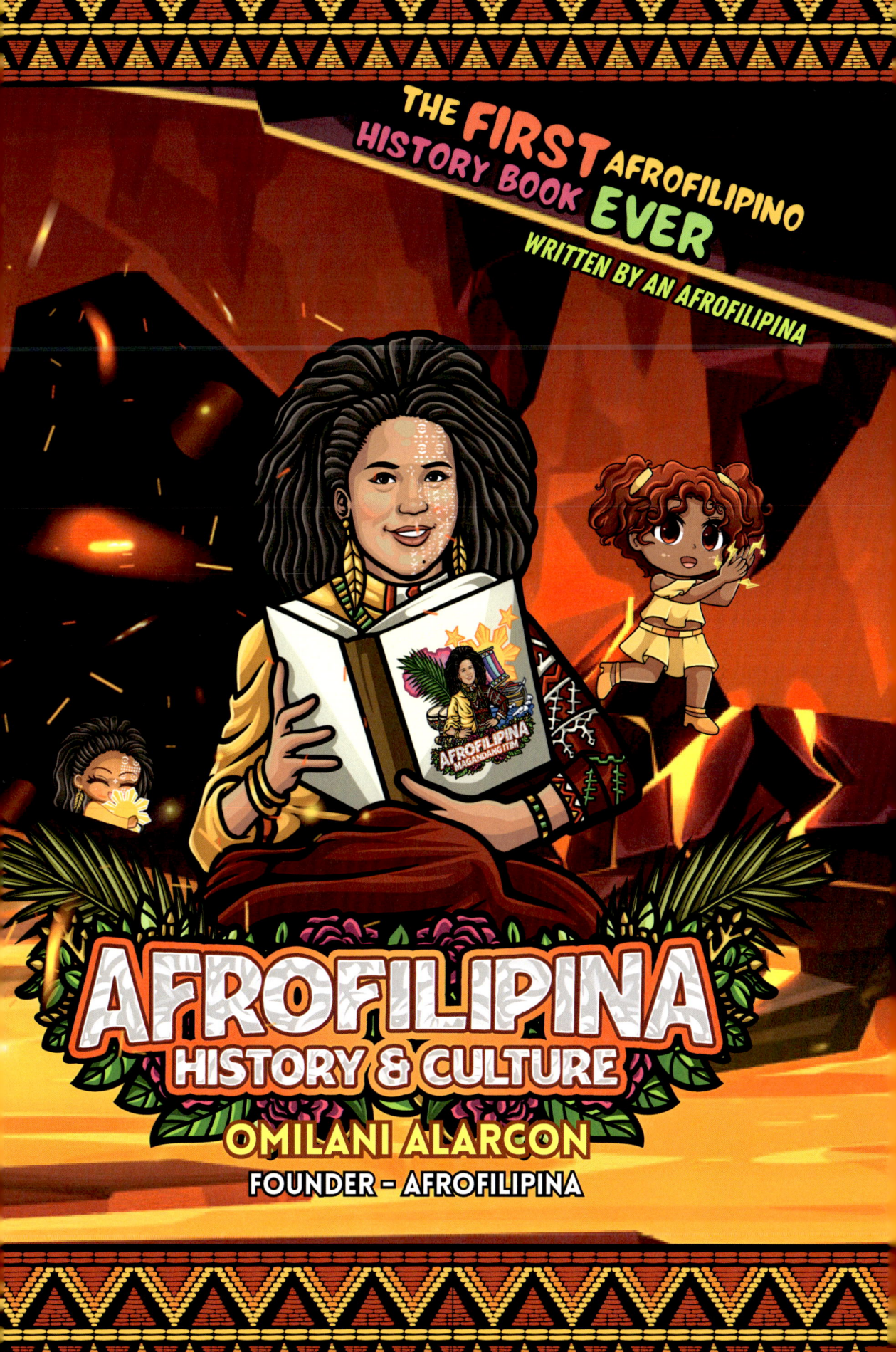

KASAYSAYAN

(HISTORY & CULTURE)

THIS HISTORY BOOK IS NOT ONE OF TIMELINES AND TALES OF WARS BETWEEN NATIONS. **AFROFILIPINA HISTORY & CULTURE** EMBRACES THE FILIPINO CONCEPT OF **KASAYSAYAN**, WHICH IS DEEPER THAN "HISTORY". KASAYSAYAN REPRESENTS THE FOLKLORE, ORAL LITERATURE, STORIES, CULTURE AND **ESSENCE** OF THE PHILIPPINES. IT IS THE STORY OF OUR PEOPLE AS TOLD AND INHERITED BY OUR PEOPLE.

KASAYSAYAN IS A TERM USED IN THE PHILIPPINES TO DESCRIBE THE STUDY OF THE NATION'S HISTORY, INCLUDING ITS PRE-COLONIAL, COLONIAL, AND POST-COLONIAL PERIODS. IT IS A HOLISTIC APPROACH THAT HIGHLIGHTS THE DISTINCTIVE EXPERIENCES, VIEWPOINTS, AND STORIES OF THE FILIPINO PEOPLE, AS WELL AS THEIR INTERACTIONS WITH DIFFERENT CULTURAL, SOCIAL, AND POLITICAL INFLUENCES.

WHAT IS BLACK?

Prior to the Trans-Atlantic Slave Trade (TAST), the term "Black" did not carry the same connotation as it does presently. In truth, Blackness did not exist as a racial category. People were identified by their ethnicities, each with their unique cultures and subcultures. Many Black people held positions of power outside of Africa.

For nearly 800 years, African Berbers known as the Moors ruled Spain. Mansa Musa and the Mali Empire were globally recognized, while the Greeks studied under Imhotep, the Egyptian multi-genius architect and physician. General Hannibal Bakar, a Black Mahout from Carthage (Tunis Africa), commanded the forces of Carthage against the Roman Republic in the Second Punic War. Hannibal Bakar was so remarkable that he was immortalized on an ancient coin, with the elephants from his battle against Rome on the other side of the coin.

MAHOUTS (S. & SE Asia) a person who works with, rides, and tends an elephant

Painting 1814 woodblock

HANNIBAL

Hannibal on Carthage (Tunis, African) coins. The Chiana Valley. Circa 208-207 BCE.

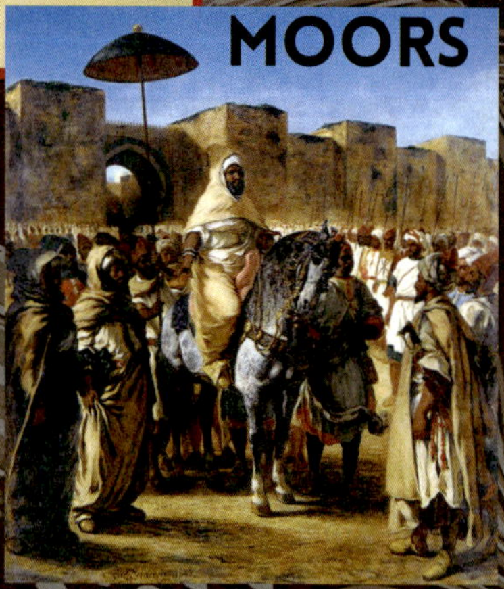

MOORS

BLACK BEGINNINGS

The contemporary racial divide, based on skin color, is a relatively recent phenomenon. It began to emerge in the last couple of centuries when racial stratification placed "white" as the superior race and people of color as inferior.

Historically, humans have enslaved each other for as long as there have been empires, states, and wars, as stated in the documentary "Stamped from the Beginning" (2023). However, before the transatlantic slave trade, the majority of enslaved people in Western European slave markets were of Eastern European descent. It was not until 1444 that the first substantial number of captive Africans were brought to Portugal to be traded and sold. According to Dr. Kendi in the documentary, these individuals were more valuable because it was harder for them to escape or blend into the population.

Black people were the targets of nefarious racial hunters and kidnappers who exploited their distinctive qualities, making them easy to identify. BLACKNESS, at that time, was utilized as a tool of enslavement and the colonial agenda for free labor and violent acquisition of power. Colonization was not a peaceful movement.

UNDERSTANDING IDENTITY IN CONTEXT

Identity encompasses much more than just belonging to a particular group. It's shaped by societal and historical factors that dictate values, hierarchies, and stereotypes beyond the boundaries of race as a social construct. One's life outcomes can be influenced by race as an economic and political factor. The ramifications of colonization and the resulting systems of oppression have had a far-reaching impact.

DIVIDE AND CONQUER

The creation of the term "Blackness" to distinguish people with dark skin from those with white skin has resulted in the perpetuation of this distinction wherever light and dark skin coexist. Throughout history, we have witnessed the repetition of this distinction in various forms of oppression, such as caste systems in India, enslavement and segregation in the Americas, apartheid in South Africa, colorism in Asia, and beyond.

It is no secret that people of color make up the majority of the world's population. If we were to come together to combat racism and oppression, we could be an unstoppable force. However, we are often given region-centric identities that encourage us to be separate and disconnected from our larger identities, except those that align with colonial agendas.

Many of the names we use to differentiate ourselves were not originally ours. For instance, the word "Asia" was an Ancient Greek term Ἀσία, first used by Herodotus (about 440 BCE) to refer to Anatolia or the Persian Empire, as opposed to Greece and Egypt. It was originally used to refer to the east bank of the Aegean Sea, an area known to the Hittites as Assuwa.

Similarly, the word "Austronesian" was assigned by German Johann Friedrich Blumenbach, who added them as the fifth category to his "varieties" of humans in the second edition of De Generis Humani Varietate Nativa (1781).

Finally, and fairly recently, the name "Denisovans" is derived from the Denisova Cave in Siberia, Russia, where the first fossils of this species were found and identified.

The common factor is that none of these names were chosen by US.

Many of the terms we use today changed constantly throughout time and were drawn among people who either had not much in common, to distinguish classes of people as separate from groups they considered inferior (like the term Filipino), or separated groups who have a lot in common but were not convenient for colonizers to group together.

Africa is one of the greatest examples where ethnic groups were lumped together who may have even had similar linguistic families but had a history of war and separate identities. This happened with so many countries and Ethnic peoples in Africa, for example as a result of the Berlin Conference (1884-1885) where there was a meeting of White Europeans to see how they would divide Africa to suit their agenda. Meetings like these occurred all over the world for centuries. This is how an extremely diverse group of people from Eastern Russia to India all the way past the Philippines all fell into a conglomerate category of Asian.

With Identity having a social context as described earlier, many Asians of today struggle with the issue of not feeling "Enough" for not fitting into the stereotype of the identity as socially and politically constructed. It is not our fault – these are not our words. We did not have meetings amongst each other to decided to unite and adapt the umbrella term.

Even if we look at the Philippines Revolution , Jose Rizal and the story of how Tagalog became our official language in resistance to Spanish colonization because it comes from our people – there are still a lot of issues. First, the people of the Philippines are NOT all TAGALOG and sadly, people use "Visaya" as an insult or turn their noses up at people not from Metro Manila or not mainstream .

No identity is perfect, but if we know where we have come from, then we can know where we are going.

BACK TO BLACK

Contrary to popular belief, misery does not love company at all. In fact people run from it and do what they can do to have the feeling of winning. This is why countries like America are obsessed with the "Dream" of opportunity and success. Across the world Black and dark skin has been treated like a burden and an undesirable trait. AntiBlackness has fueled the skin bleaching industry, being the inspiration for the dream of marrying "up" a euphemism for marrying white. In Latin America, for example, it is called "mejorando la raza" (improving the race). People whisper to their daughters to never marry dark and treat Blackness so violently.

It affects our identity and the way we seek history. For example, I feel that some people adapt to the Denisovan theory to avoid ties to being Black , but surprise! The group of people with the highest Denisovan DNA are Black. Science has also proven that the adaptations made by the Denisovans to advance and become their species happened in West Africa.

Division and denial keeps us conquered. Black and Brown people all over the world have suffered discrimination, have had to fight through economic barriers while still somehow managing to smile through it all. We all have the stereotype of being the happiest people and so giving and caring. This is part of our stereotype as is the idea that we are somehow primitive, archaic, and in need of saving while being exploited.

Filipinos were and still are treated BLACK. Indigenous Filipinos like Aeta groups are treated BLACK. There is nothing wrong with being BLACK. BLACK has been hurt BLACK is overworked and undervalued, but BLACK IS still BEAUTIFUL and WE ARE BEAUTIFUL. WE ARE BEAUTIFULLY BLACK AND BROWN.

DENISOVAN

  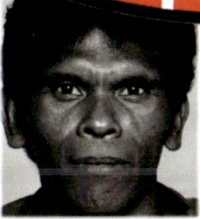 

   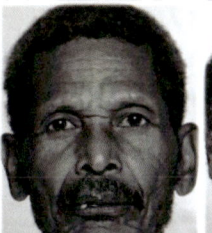 

Home/News & Opinion

Indigenous Filipino Group Has Highest Known Denisovan Ancestry

Researchers found the relatively high proportion of DNA from a hominin cousin—nearly 5 percent—when they scanned more than 1,000 genomes from 118 distinct ethnic groups.

Annie Melchor
Aug 13, 2021 | 3 min read

Register for free to listen to this article

Listen with Speechify
0:00

PDF VERSION

Share:

U ntil recently, scientists thought the modern humans with the highest proportion of Denisovan ancestry lived in Papua New Guinea and Australia. According to a new study published yesterday (August 12) in *Current Biology*, however, an Indigenous group in the Philippines called the Ayta Magbukon have 30 to 40 percent more Denisovan DNA than these other frontrunners, for a total of nearly 5 percent of their genomes.

ABOVE: Self-identified Negritos from various islands of the Philippines.
© AMELIA PERSSON

Denisovans were a group of archaic humans, named from a single finger bone found in a Siberian cave. They coexisted with modern humans and other archaic human species, such as Neanderthals, and interbred with those groups until they went extinct an estimated 30,000 to 50,000 years ago. According to *Popular Mechanics*, Pacific Islanders and Southeast Asians have substantial Denisovan ancestry in their genomes, while people in other parts of Asia have less than 0.05 percent Denisovan ancestry. People of African and European descent don't have any.

"[The Ayta Magbukon] have more Denisovan ancestry than anybody else on the planet today," Uppsala University biologist and study coauthor Mattias Jakobsson tells *Inverse*. "So that was a surprise."

See "Humans Made . . . . than 40,000 Years"

According to *Gizmodo*, the authors were originally interested in studying the peoples of the Philippines as part of a massive collaboration with Indigenous communities, the Commission for Culture and the Arts of the Philippines, researchers at the University.

As a follow-up study to one studying human migration to the Philippines, we intended to look at the distant past by assessing the levels of archaic ancestry among the populations, especially as populations in these regions were previously shown to have high levels of Denisovan ancestry, and Southeast Asia is known to be inhabited by various archaic species," population geneticist and study coauthor Maximilian Larena tells *Gizmodo*.

FILIPINO SUPERSTITIONS

These are just a few interesting superstitions found in some cultures in the Philippines

ALWAYS GIVE MONEY WHEN SOMEONE GIVES SHOES AS A GIFT

SAY TABI TABI PO WHEN ENTERING THE FOREST

NEVER OPEN AN UMBRELLA IN THE HOUSE

SLIPPERS BY THE DOOR WARD OFF UNWELCOME SPIRITS.

DREAMS HAVE MESSAGES AND MEANINGS

WHISTLING AT NIGHT CALLS SPIRITS

PANCIT BRINGS LONG LIFE

PLAYING ISUNGKA INDOORS CAN BRING BAD LUCK

A NOTE ABOUT "FILIPINO" MYTHOLOGY

The first thing to know about Filipino Mythology is that there is no such thing. Let me explain. With over 7,000 islands and over 104 ethnic groups, Filipino identity is far from monolithic. There is no homogenous Filipino way, although a shared history connects us. Even on islands beliefs and practices vary.

As I researched Filipino myths, I was confused about why I was getting so many variations in details or descriptions about the mythological stories so I reached out to Owen Layungan, an expert in Pre-Colonial Philippine History. As per the conversation, he emphasized the significance of understanding the nuances of each island and ethnic group when exploring the region's history.

As such, I would like to share some stories I have come across while delving into the topic. It is important to note that these tales vary in detail and gender assignments depending on the location and people sharing the story. My sources include interviews, childhood anecdotes, and research. I have selected stories that resonate with my experience as an AfroFilipina.

As I wrote the AfroFilipina History & Culture book, I felt inexplicably drawn towards a volcano, and being inside the volcano became a symbolic representation that I am still seeking to understand. The more I researched Kan-Laon and Lalahon, the more I began to see some correlations. Sometimes, I feel like a guardian of a volcanic crater defending the land from those who wish to exploit our fertile soil. Other times, I feel at home within the protection of the volcano's turbulent chambers, amidst the molten rock, magma, lava and volcanic ash plumes.

The Malakas (Strength) at Maganda (Beauty) creation story is another tale that both fascinates and troubles me, despite its problematic ending. These stories, rooted in my own homelands and people, resonate with me in a profound way.

Worldwide for generations, people have talked about the Romans and the Greeks - their mythology and astrology. But when the lore comes from your own homelands and your own people, "it hits differently". The more I learn, the more I love all that we are through the calm and the storm.

As I piece together these stories, I feel as though I am gaining insight into my ancestral past and perhaps even a roadmap for our future.

PRECOLONIAL SPIRITUALITY

In my understanding, Anito, or Diwata as it is referred to in the Visayas and Mindanao, symbolizes not only the spiritual forces present in nature but also the precolonial spiritual practices of our people. It represents the divine manifestation in all living things. Unfortunately, our traditional practices were often misinterpreted as evil or ungodly. Protective devices and amulets were labeled as fetish, and Baybaylan (spiritualists who held onto their traditional beliefs) were either viewed as heathens and marginalized or were exoticized by foreigners. One of the primary objectives of colonization was to replace the power structure from images and symbols that reflect the people to thos who held onto their traditional beliefs) were either viewed as heathens and marginalized or were exoticized by foreigners. One of the primary objectives of colonization is to replace the power structure from images and symbols that reflect the people to those favoringe favoring the colonizers. Not just in the Philippines – people of color worldwide were taught that their ancestral customs are evil, while the colonizers' belief system was imposed was imposed on them.on them.

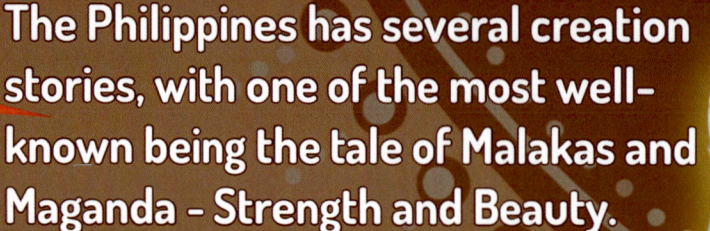

The Philippines has several creation stories, with one of the most well-known being the tale of Malakas and Maganda - Strength and Beauty.

The narrative unfolds during a period when the Earth was devoid of land and only the sky and sea existed. Manaul, a mythological bird flying the landless earth, grew restless from ceaseless flight as there was no place to land. In frustration, he unleashed a powerful flap of his wings, causing a storm between the sky and the sea.

The fight between the sky and the seas shook up everything and islands began to rise from the ocean forming the Philippine Islands. Now Manaul was able to walk on land. While Manaul was enjoying the new solid ground and dancing between the seas and the shore, bamboo washed across the shore and struck Manaul on his leg.

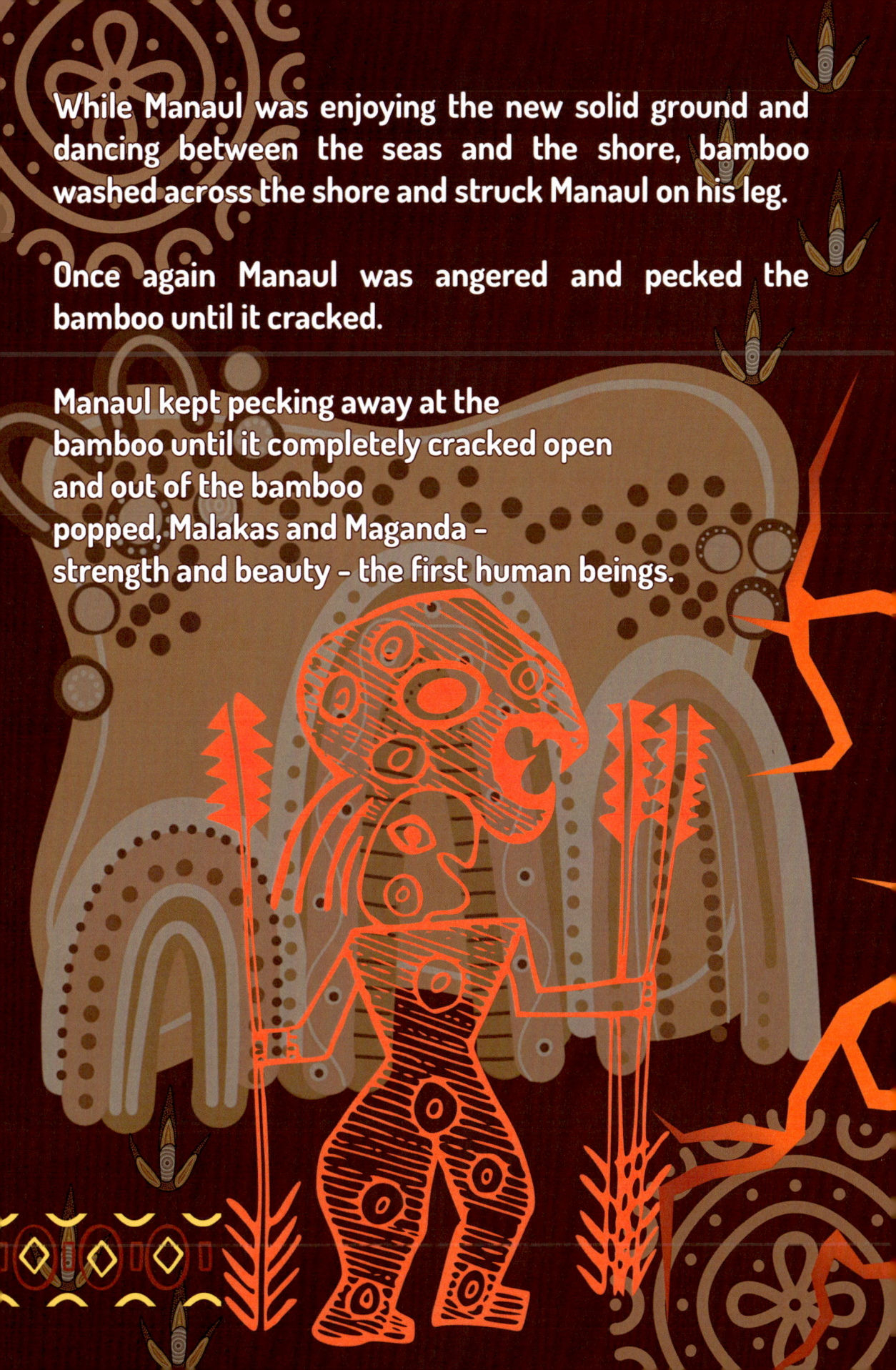

While Manaul was enjoying the new solid ground and dancing between the seas and the shore, bamboo washed across the shore and struck Manaul on his leg.

Once again Manaul was angered and pecked the bamboo until it cracked.

Manaul kept pecking away at the bamboo until it completely cracked open and out of the bamboo popped, Malakas and Maganda – strength and beauty – the first human beings.

MALAKAS AT MAGANDA
... but wait, there's more

Malakas at Maganda multiplied and had many children that misbehaved a lot. One day Malakas (Strength) was chasing the children to discipline them and they ran in different directions.

One group ran into the hidden rooms of the house and became the Timawa (chiefs), another group ran into the walls and became Alipin (slaves) while others ran outside and were free people Maharlikas, while others hid in the fireplace and became dark-skinned Aetas. Another group fled to the sea and were gone for many years and returned as white tourists.

NOTE:

As an AfroFilipina, certain parts of this story are deeply unsettling. The transformation of the Aetas' skin color to black after being burnt in fire and the tourists' change to white men raises questions. Why did this have to happen or be explained this way? Who started this story?

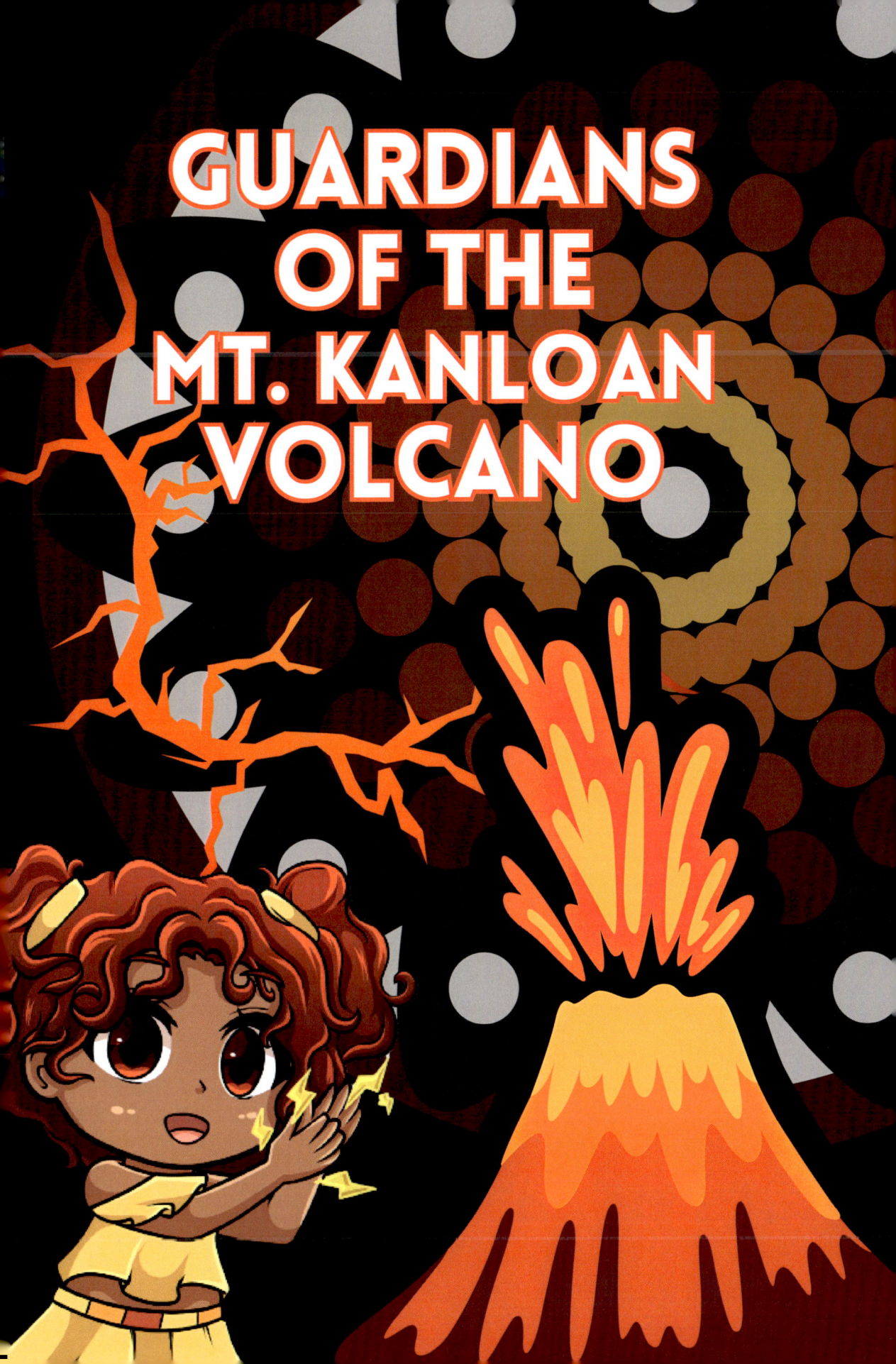

NEGROS

If we ever doubt who we are, just remember there is a whole island called **NEGROS**. It is the **fourth largest** and third most populous island in the Philippines. The inhabitants are called Negrenses or Negrosanons.

In **1565** Spanish Colonizers called the island **NEGROS** because they were met with a large population of **Black people**. The name remains today.

NEGROS ←

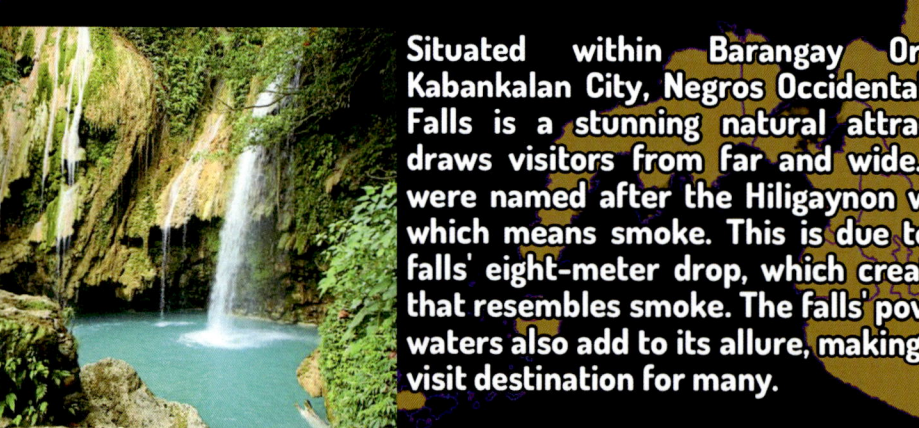

Situated within Barangay Oringao in Kabankalan City, Negros Occidental, Mag-Aso Falls is a stunning natural attraction that draws visitors from far and wide. The falls were named after the Hiligaynon word "aso," which means smoke. This is due to the twin falls' eight-meter drop, which creates a mist that resembles smoke. The falls' powdery blue waters also add to its allure, making it a must-visit destination for many.

FACES OF NEGROS

via Harvard University
PEABODY MUSEUM of
Archaeology & Ethnology

Visayan women of Negros Occidental
William Cameron Forbes 1891 - 1912

The Bukidnon of Negros
W. C. Forbes 1891 - 1912

INTERESTING FACTS ABOUT VOLCANOES

1. **Volcanoes are named after Vulcan,** Roman God of Fire
2. **Volcanoes produce some of the most nutrient rich soil**
3. Magma and Lava are not the same – Magma is the molten liquid rock that exists under the Earth's surface. It contains dissolved gasses, and when the pressure reaches a certain point and the gasses expand, there is an explosion at the mouth of a volcano. Once it reaches the surface and is expelled from the volcano, it becomes lava. Although there are three types of lava — basaltic, andesitic and rhyolitic, they all contain silica.
4. Pumice stones that people use in spas come from volcanic igneous rock. Pumice is a unique volcanic rock (igneous) that can float in water. It can also be used as an abrasive and is sometimes used in beauty salons for removing dry skin.
5. A volcano is an opening in the Earth's surface. Usually found in a mountain, the opening allows gas, hot magma and ash to escape from beneath the Earth's crust.
6. Volcanoes don't just occur on land. They can be found on the ocean floor and under ice caps, too!
7. Lava from a volcano can reach 1,250°C! Lava is so hot it can burn everything in its path. If you used a glass thermometer to take the temperature it would melt!

KAN-LAON

Kanlaon was named after Kan-Laon, the supreme god of the region known as the "god of time". Bathala, the supreme god in Tagalog mythology, was his counterpart. According to the most popular legend, Kan-Laon regarded the mountain as his personal garden, which was tended to by farmers he trusted not to trespass. However, during one of his extended travels, the farmers, fearing he would never return, began to encroach on his territory, and eventually, began converting it into farmland. Upon his return, Kan-Laon was enraged, and in his fury, caused the once-peaceful garden to erupt, destroying the farms and surrounding areas. Kan-Laon then sealed off his garden and was never seen again. Since that fateful day, Mt. Kanlaon has erupted regularly, serving as a reminder of Kan-Laon's righteous anger. However, many believe that Kan-Laon will eventually return to calm the mountain and restore it to its former glory.

KAN-LAON
INTERESTING FACTS

1. Kanlaon started off as a mountain that Kan-Laon turned into a volcano

2. Kanlaon was an elderly man who lived in a hut at the peak of the volcano.

3. Many perform rituals and sacred magic on the mountains and see the peak of the volcano where Kan-Laon lived as sacred. Many people take pilgrimages to the volcano and traverse the forest burning incense and searching for herbs.

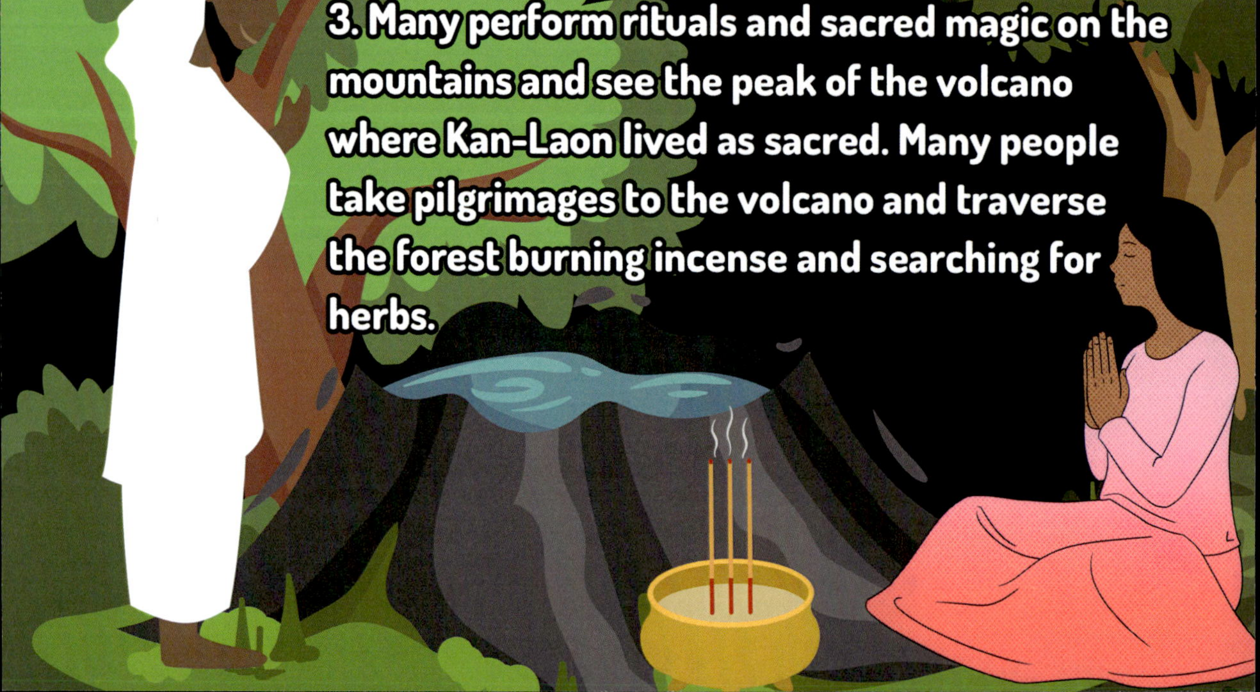

Deep within Mt. Kanlaon's dense forest lived the magkupo - a colossal serpent with a rooster's crown and a powerful crow. It resided beneath the kamandag tree, near the volcano's crater. With fins on its sides, the magkupo was unique in that it didn't slither on the ground like other snakes, but rather moved from tree to tree by coiling its long body around the trunk and extending its head to reach the next one. The name "magkupó" was derived from its coiling movements, which resemble an embrace or an effect of sticking-on to something. Hidden in the forest canopy, the magkupo waits patiently to deter evil individuals who disturb the peace of Kan-Laon.

MAGKUPO

Many of us yearn to discover the ways of our ancestors before colonization. However, our traditions were not easily relinquished. Rather, there was significant resistance and a rejection of colonialism. In fact, traditional healers, known as Babaylans, fled to the mountains and became maroons, creating new communities and leaving their old ones behind. The survival of so many Kan-Laon stories is a testament to our people and their perseverance against colonization. Despite the Spanish conquistadores' attempts to convert loyal followers through the introduction of Christianity, the worship of Kan-Laon remained strong and widespread throughout Negros Island.

LALAHON
Bisayan Goddess of Agriculture, Harvests, & Protectress of Mt. Kanlaon

Lalahon, a legendary diwata from ancient Visayan folktales and written myths, has undergone significant transformations over the years due to Spanish influences. She is known as the goddess of harvests, the guardian of Mount Kanlaon volcano, and the goddess who protects against natural disasters caused by volcanic eruptions, wildfires, and earthquakes.

While some sources describe Lalahon as male, the ancient Negrense groups residing near Mount Kanlaon believe that volcanoes resemble women: sometimes quiet, serene, and beautiful, but also capable of being fierce, destructive, and violent during eruptions. Thus, many stories portray Lalahon as a woman.

Lalahon represents the gateway to the Upper Heavens, while Kan-Laon symbolizes the Upper Heavens themselves. The tobacco plant is sacred to Lalahon, as well as to Kanlaon, and her favorite animal is the Visayan spotted deer, which is currently endangered and near extinction, and can only be found in Negros. The fire tree is believed to be her tree, and in ancient times, Babaylans would enter a trance using sacred herbs and intoxicating "tuba" (moonshine) under the tree or near the volcano's crater to gain wisdom from this remarkable diwata.

DEEPER MEANING

Filipino history has always linked spirituality with the earth and its governing forces. As such, the Diwata (gods) from Aeta, such as Kan-Laon and Lalahon, can be seen as Black Indigenous gods. Many Filipinos hold deeply spiritual beliefs and superstitions.

The stories of Malakas and Maganda, as well as Kan-Laon and Lalahon, illustrate a balance between male and female energies that complement each other in different ways.

Personally, I can relate to Kan-Laon's generosity and have felt the sting of giving my all and having it taken for granted. Like Lalahon, I remain vigilant and protective of those around me. Being AfroFilipina feels like balancing on the edge of a volcano, watching for any encroachment on my fertile land. While volcanoes are dangerous, they also produce some of the most fertile soil in the world. This contrast is what defines my everyday life.

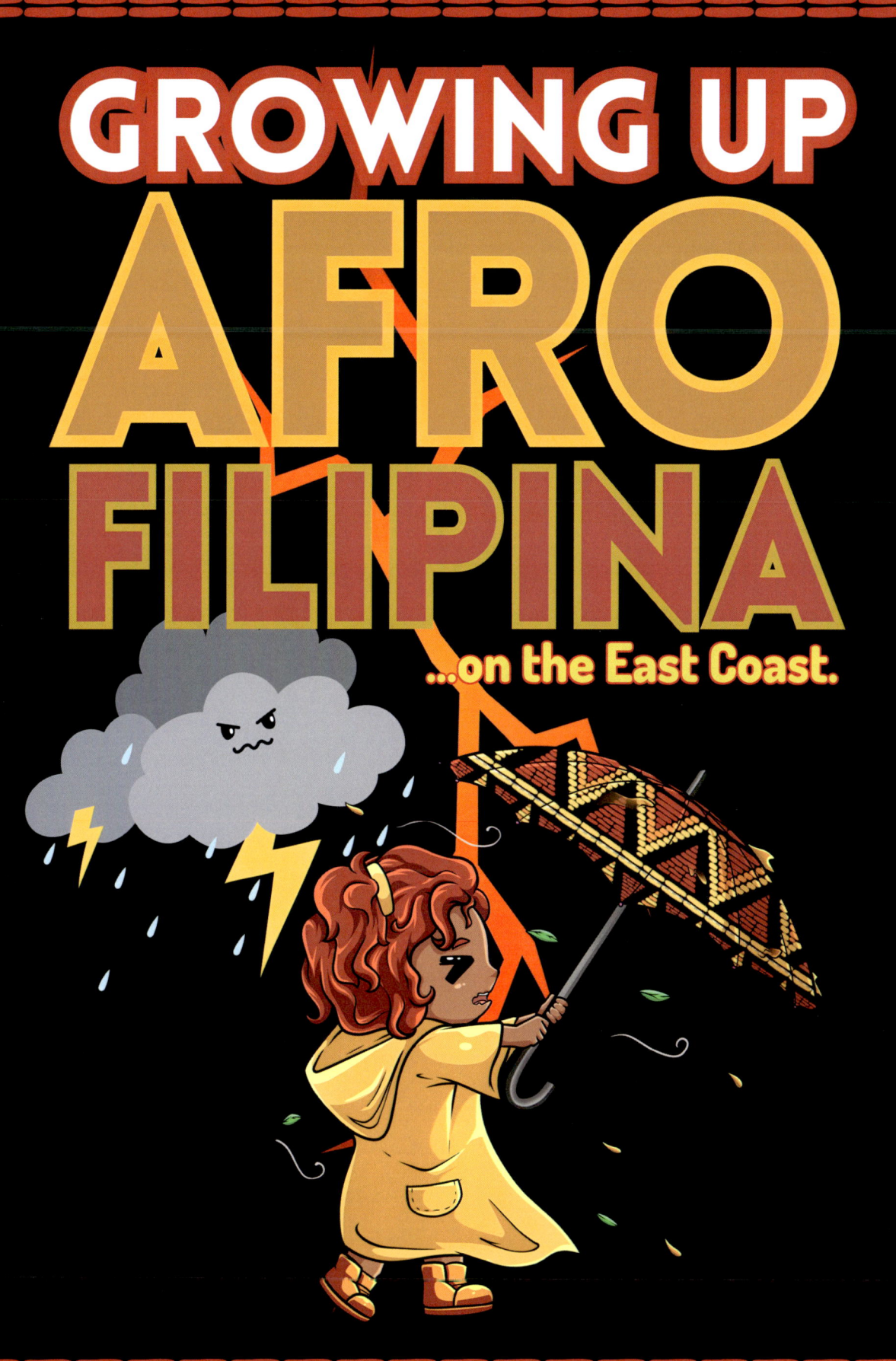

This is the history book I always wish I had. This is the history book I always wish I had. This is the history book I always wish I had. This is the history book I always wish I had. This is the history..

If you are reading this and you are also AfroFilipino, then you **know** why this line **repeats**. Everywhere we go, the feeling of alienation and rejection follows us. Yet, I would not trade being **AFROFILIPINA** for anything. Life has not been easy.

I grew up on the East Coast of the United States, at the time there were very few Filipinos. The small community in North Carolina was comprised of mainly new arrivals. Walking into a room with my AfroFilipino/AfroPuerto Rican family - **heads would turn** -**eyes would roll** - and a thick, uncomfortable **silence** would drape over the room. There was always an unspoken feeling of "why are you here" ?!? It used to bother me until I realized **why** they were looking at me so strangely.

Thankfully, my innocence protected me. My 5 year old mind decided that the people were mean because they did not know I was Filipina. As a resourceful child I figured that they wouldn't know I was Filipina because I did not have on a "Maria Clara dress". From that moment, I dreamed of having my own Maria Clara dress so I could be **seen** as a Filipina.

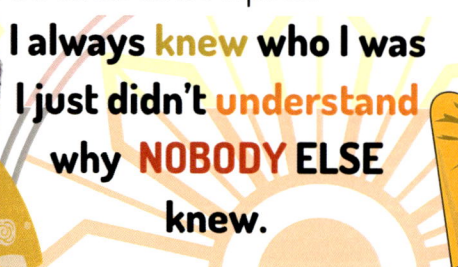

I always **knew** who I was
I just didn't **understand**
why **NOBODY ELSE**
knew.

Once I was older, I was finally able to purchase my first Filipiniana dress. It was a custom dress from the Philippines – fancy and hand painted, made of the pineapple fiber and I felt like putting on this dress was like draping myself in my roots and culture. I anxiously anticipated the moment to show off my new beautiful dress from the mother land.

When I finally debuted, I strutted like a runway model and the runway quickly transformed into a walk of shame because my joy was met with unwelcoming stares, and something underscribable that is beyond "shade". AfroFilipinos will know this uneasy look and feeling. What I was not prepared for is the unwelcoming comments.

I have been told, "**Whatever else you are, that is what you are**" or "**You are NOT Filipina**" or "**Are you sure?**".

I have had doors slammed in my face, been cut out of pictures, people turned their back to me while I was singing.

I never experienced the Jim Crow south but every time I went into Filipino spaces I felt the heaviness of racism and segregation. Some of these people were the same complexion as me. I was treated as if my **Blackness** is a crime.

This is why I say **MAGANDANG ITIM (Black is Beautiful)**, because nobody has ever said it in Tagalog... because when people read it on my bag or my page they frown their faces. Why is it so hard to see **BLACK** as **BEAUTIFUL**? Why is the rejection of BLACK Filipinos so emotionally violent?

Being AfroFilipina is traumatic. Like many people, I got so fed up with the rejection and the absurdly nasty way people treat us that I decided to erase my identity. I began to hate being Filipino to the point that seeing Filipino people or anything related to the Philippines was a form of PTSD. I mean that my body physically reacted to all things Filipino.

I happily embraced the fact that I was **BLACK ONLY** and that I would be perfectly fine **NEVER** identifying as Filipina again... at least that was the plan.

Some things in life are much larger than our plans. I would learn this lesson much later and after going on a quest to Puerto Rico to see if I would be more at peace identifying as Puerto Rican. I made a documentary about the experience.

Whatchu mean I don't look Filipino? I have been told that so many times, I don't "look" Filipino and yet each time someone says that, I just freeze. I don't know what to say. We get so used to letting things slide because first there is the shock of the audacity that someone would say something so evil to another human being and then the hurt sets in when you realize what they are really saying. It cuts deep, so it's too painful to address it in the moment. I just want to say ----

IT IS SO RUDE AND DISRESPECTFUL TO SAY THAT!

IT'S NOT OK

Plus it's very ignorant
Because if you knew what a

FILIPINO

was, you'd realize
you don't look Filipino either

FILIPINOS

To understand "**Filipino**", you have to start with colonization and the exploitation of our lands. The "**Philippines**" was not even the **first** choice, it was a **strategic choice** of the colonial agenda. The Spaniards positioned themselves in the Philippines to gain easy access into an area once called, "The East Indies or the  "Spice Islands" (The Malay Archipelago). In March 1521, Portuguese navigator and "explorer" (colonizer), Ferdinand Magellan sailed under a Spanish flag and landed on the coast of Cebu. Our **ancestors fought** with all their might to **resist** the efforts and agenda of the colonizers. As legend has it, the **Datu** warrior **Lapu Lapu** - Chief of **Mactan** in the Visayas, defeated the Spanish forces on April 26, 1521. The Spanish did not return to the Philippines unti 40 years later.

In **1543**, the islands were named the Philippines in honor of the crown prince **Philip**. His son, Philip II, inherited the lands and the islands were officially named for him. Notably, the name Philippines was initially **only intended** for Leyte, Samar, and other adjacent islands.

Furthermore, everyone was not Filipino. There was a **distinction** between the **Spaniards** and those indigenous to the islands.

The people that are envisioned when saying "**Filipino**" today were called Indios, Indigena or Chinos by the Spaniards. There is also documentation of the use of the term Indios Filipinos or Chinos Filipinos to make a distinction between the people they identified under the same names in the Caribbean, South America and in North America.

The name shifted again in the **19th Century** when Filipino was used as a distinction to identify Philippine-born **Spaniards**. Initially they were called Españoles Filipinos, and then just Filipino, to distinguish them from the Spaniards born in Spain. They also resented this term because they too did not want to be distinct from the people of their homeland.

Movements, revolutions and literature of the late 19th and early 20th century made yet another shift as **Mestizo Filipinos** (mixed with indigenous and other ancestry) and **ilustrados** (Filipino elitist intellectual class), including Filipino national hero, Jose Rizal, sought to reclaim the Filipino identity to include everyone born in the islands (Kramer, 2006).

Our ancestors fought against colonial agenda and the type of separation people perpetuate today.

JOSE RIZÁL

IT MAKES ME WONDER. WOULD THE GATEKEEPING FILIPINOS HAVE JOINED MAGELLAN OR WOULD THEY STAND AGAINST COLONIZATION WITH LAPU LAPU?

This is why I founded AfroFilipina, both because I was fed up with being treated like an outcast and because we need people to advocate for us. We need better advocacy and support around the emotional, intellectual and social trauma we encounter in our interactions with the Filipino community.

At the same time, I have heard some of these same concerns expressed by Diaspora Filipinos all over the world. Especially those who didn't grow up in the islands or who have been here a while. This is why AfroFilipina is a space of learning, sharing, and advocacy for the Filipino community in general. I am on a mission to uncover our history, origins, and to decolonize while un-learning all we have been mis-informed about.

As you can see, the history and the path to our identity is complicated. Throughout history colonizers and people in power have sought to redefine their territories and assign meanings and values that are mainly for the purpose of protecting their assets and increasing power, domination and control. The forced identities had nothing to do with the actual people of the lands and their culture.

This is why debate so today about who we are and who is entitled to the identity. The same was done in the United States as they developed racial categories, of which there are 5 at the time of writing this book:

1. **White**
2. **Black** or African American
3. **Native Hawaiian** or Other **Pacific Islander**
4. **Asian**
5. **Indigenous** – American Indian or Alaska Native

These categories are also classified as Hispanic/non Hispanic. In the book **Latinos of Asia** (Ocampo: 2016), Ocampo addresses how the racial categories were assigned and chosen in the mid-late 20th century. Our cultural nuances were not taken into account and people with such a wide range of identities, linguistic families and culture were all lumped into the same category – **Asian**. These categories do not reflect how we navigate the world and many of us find ourselves lost in the boxes and check marks assigned to us. This point is further compounded by the fact that reclaiming a **FILIPINO** identity in the United States has a different meaning than it has in the Philippines government standard definition.

This is why we debate so much today about who we are and who is privy to the identity. Race, Nationality and Ethnicity are important distinctions.

RACIALLY – we are Asian or BLASIAN this is based on the US categorization of the 5 racial categories. Similar categories may exist other places in the world.

NATIONALITY – is based on a person's birthplace, domicile and citizenship status. If you are American born or naturalized, your nationality is **AMERICAN**.

ETHNICITY – is has to do with a shared ancestral land and roots regardless of the place of birth and based on:

> perceived shared attributes that distinguish them from other groups. Those attributes can include a common nation of origin, or common sets of ancestry, traditions, language, history, society, religion, or social treatment (kanchan 2012: 69 - 70)

(Chandra, Kanchan (2012). Constructivist theories of ethnic politics. Oxford University Press. pp. 69-70.

This point will be further important later on as I discuss the meaning of AFROFILIPINA. For now, this explains the frequent debates about who is/is not Filipino.

A person can be born in Canada (Nationality), racially Asian and Ethnically Filipino. In addition, there is also personal choice! A person may not feel they connect with their national culture and identity and prefer to honor the identity of their ancestors. Claiming Filipino identity is just as personal and political as it is governmental and statistical. These are the nuances of everyday life.

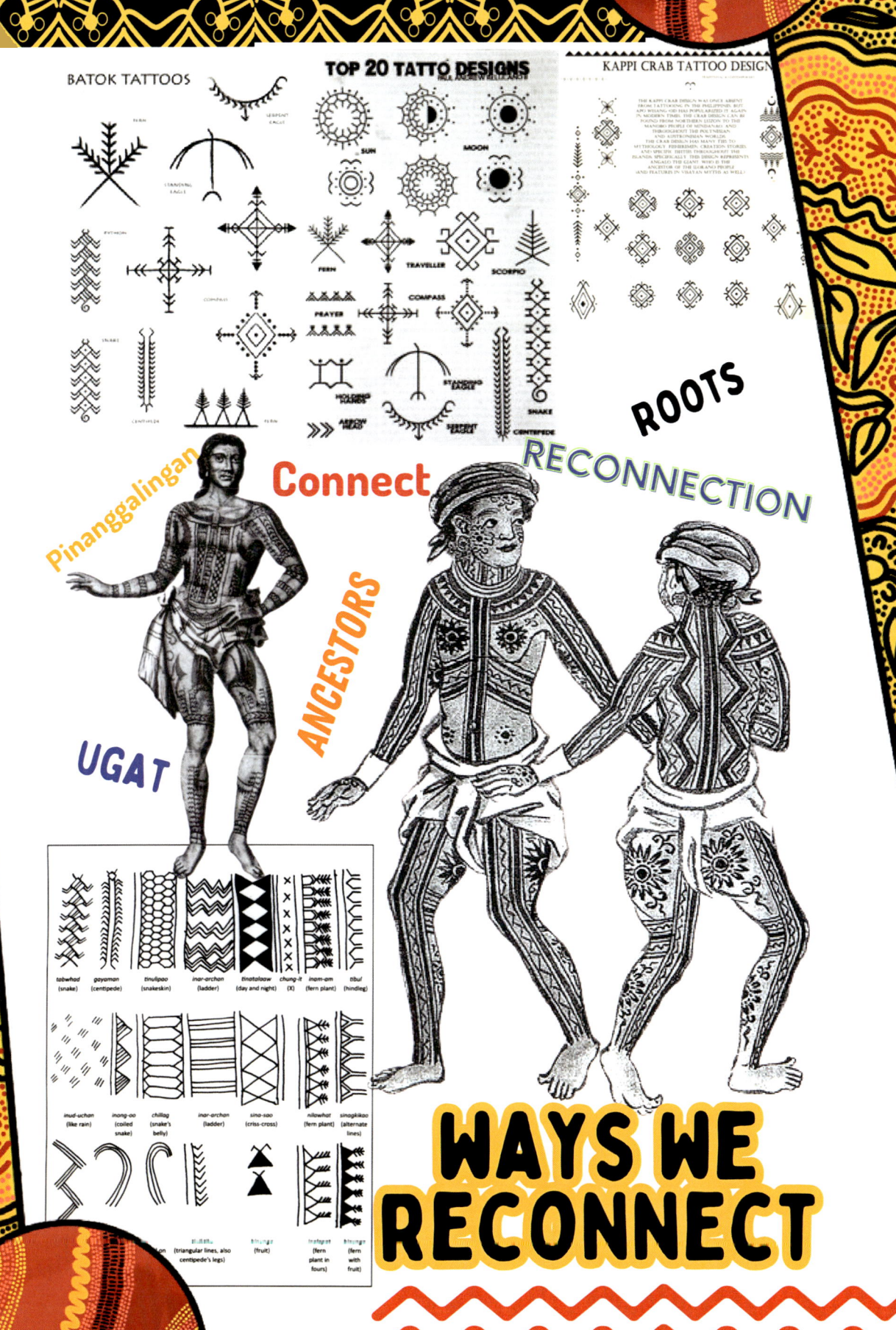

BATOK
TRADITIONAL TATTOO Ways we reconnect

Like me, many of you are just beginning to learn about and embrace your Filipino culture, history and identity. In our search for our ancestral lands we do all kinds of things to reconnect. One of the debates and popular ways of reconnection is through the tradtional tattoos - Batok.

Vogue magazine broke the internet and the news stands with their historic front cover featuring the legendary 106 year old Kalinga Tattoo traditionalist - Apo Whang-Od. People come from all over the world to get one of her famous tattoos done in the old tradition. She is documented as the last mambabatok of her generation.

Traditionally the tattoos had a very sacred meaning and had to be earned.

This is not to say the tattoos of today are not meaningful. I just mean that people have different motivations for getting the tattoos. For some it is an iconic thing to do as a souvenir of traveling to a unique space and for others it represents the ancestors and connecting with our past traditions. Sometimes we do not know where to begin to connect with our Filipino side and for many, the tattoos are part of that journey.

FOOD

For diasporan Filipinos, food serves as a means of connection and reconnection to our roots. Many of the ingredients utilized in our dishes reflect the diversity of the islands -- Fresh coconut and Lechon, crispy Turon on banana leaves -- A taste of Filipino cuisine can transport one to the islands, connecting them to our amazing culture and its rich history. In my experience, whenever I found myself in a place where there were no visible Filipino communities, I sought out Filipino restaurants and Asian markets to reconnect with my heritage through the food.

Kamayan Lunch at Lutong Pinoy II - Pembroke Pines, FL
With Restaraunt owner Darren Mendoza - Nanay Meddy
and Dr. Gel Cortez Founder of LEAD Filipino

Lutong Pinoy in Pembroke Pines, FL was always home for me. The cuisine transported me back to my ancestral roots, allowing me to stay connected with my culture, my people, and the spirit of generosity. It is a space where I saw community come together with an unparalleled level of support and solidarity.

Our people have some of the most fantastic tapestry in the world. We are **master weavers** and have done the wonder of changing pineapple and banana fibers into beautiful cloth. Our ancestors are geniuses.

The most fascinating weavers to me are the ones who come from the region of my Ancestors in Mindanao. The T'Boli tribe weaves a cloth called **T'nalak** which is the art of dream weaving and that is exactly what it sounds like. It is a very spiritual process where, for more than 300 years, women have woven patterns inspired by visions given to them by the goddess, Fu Dalu (the spirit of abaca). The weaving is a sacred tribute to the goddess and the process can take 3 to 4 months.

The cloth was very spiritual and used both for offerings and as a means of acquiring resources. The cloth was used to barter in trade and at times also denoted status and wealth. It is amazing to fathom how versatile, spiritual and symbolic the T'nalak cloth has been. In the article, "T'Nalak: The Land of the Dreamweavers" (David and Everett: 2020) the authors explain:

> **The T'nalak reflects core themes that can be used to understand Filipino American studies, including bayanihan and damay, which are examples of strong community partnership as participant or recipient. The whole process of T'nalak weaving, from dyeing to weaving, is descended from generation to generation of maternal relatives that necessitated a community of woven fabrics and traditional plant based-dying in order to sustain the tradition of T'nalak weaving. By creating specific coloration and subsets of T'nalak, it also provides signs of Filipino cultural identity, rank, and status.**

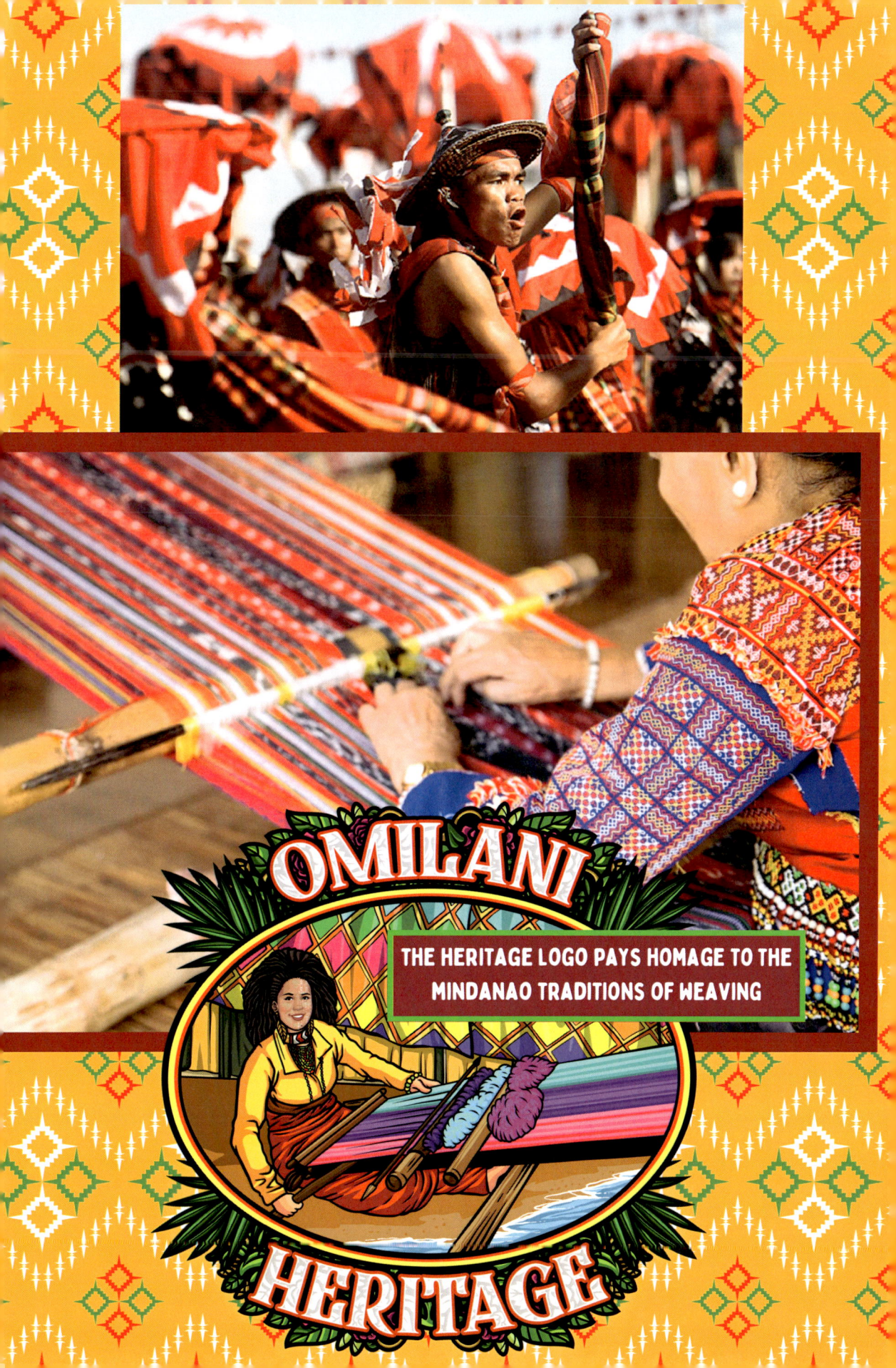

A HYDROGRAPHICAL AND CHOROGRAPHICAL CHART OF THE PHILIPPINES, DRAWN BY THE JESUIT FATHER PEDRO MURILLO VELARDE (1696-1753) AND PUBLISHED IN MANILA IN 1734.

FILIPINO ANCESTRAL BELIEFS

There are many cultural practices and ancestral beliefs in the Philippines. I will share just a few that may be found in different cultures. Practices will vary throughout the more than 7,000 islands of the Philippines.

1. Lighting a candle for the departed Ancestors.
2. Setting aside food at the table for the ancestor.
3. Visiting the cemetary and sitting a while with family at the burial plot. Sometimes with food and chairs.
4. Belief that the spirits of the Ancestors visit or leave signs.
5. If you are "haunted" by the spirit, sometimes water or something will be left for them so the person will not be troubled by the spirit.
6. Don't go straight home after a funeral or wake

Some Tagalog people traditionally believe in two forms of the soul:
- **KAKAMBAL** (twin) – the soul of the living. It is believed that Every time a person sleeps, the kakambal may travel.
- **KALULUWA** (spirit) – after one dies the kaluluwa travels to either Kasanaan (like hell) or Maca (heaven)
- There also exists a tradition called pangangaluluwa that helps ancestors to arrive peacefully to Maca or gives an opportunity for redemption of those sent to kasanaan.

Maitum Burial Pottery

The significance of these artifacts is that they were not located until 1991. They were found in Maitum Mindanao and estimated to a calibrated date of 190 BC to 500 AD. Also significant is the attention to detail. Some of the pottery had expressions of happiness, sadness, or shock. They were adorned with beads or jewelry and were made to look like the image of the body they were guarding.

AETA 1938
SOURCE: JOHN TEWELL EICKSTEDT - EGON, GERMANY EAST ASIA EXPEDITION 1937/1939 DEUTSCHE FOTOTHEK DRESDEN MUSEUM OF ETHNOLOGY, GERMANY

ANCESTORS

WE ALSO RECONNECT WITH OUR ROOTS THROUGH OUR ANCESTORS AND LIVING ELDERS. I AM SO THANKFUL TO MY ANCESTORS FOR CONTINUING THE KNOWLEDGE OF THE PHILIPPINES AND MY HERITAGE IN ZAMBOANGA AND BATANGAS. I LEARNED MY HISTORY THROUGH MY GRANDMOTHER'S VIVID RETELLING OF MY GRANDFATHER'S CAPTURE IN JAPAN, AS WELL AS HER TALES OF THE MOROS AND ZAMBOANGA. EVERYTHING FASCINATED ME. HER ANIMATED NARRATION LED ME TO BELIEVE THAT HER STORIES WERE WORKS OF FICTION. HOWEVER, WHEN I EMBARKED ON A QUEST TO LOCATE MY FAMILY IN THE PHILIPPINES, MY GRANDMOTHER'S STORIES PROVED TO BE ACCURATE. IT IS A TESTAMENT TO THE VALUE OF OUR KASAYSAYAN (FOLKLORIC HISTORY). OUR ANCESTORS AND ELDERS POSSESS A WEALTH OF KNOWLEDGE AND ARE THE LAST REMAINING INDIVIDUALS TO HAVE WITNESSED THE EVENTS THEY DESCRIBE. THEY ARE WALKING HISTORY BOOKS.

MY GRANDPARENTS & FATHER

KASAYSAYAN AS A ROADMAP

LIKE A RECORD ON REPLAY, MY GRANDMOTHER REPEATED THE SAME STORIES OVER AND OVER. ONE WOULD THINK IT WOULD BE EXHAUSTING TO HEAR THE SAME STORY, BUT I CLUNG TO EVERY WORD AND WAS DETERMINED TO REMEMBER ALL THE DETAILS.

THE ANCESTORS WERE ALIVE IN THE WORLD OF MY GRANDMOTHER AND THEREFORE THEY WERE ALSO LIVING TO ME. I KNEW THE PERSONALITIES, THE JOYS AND THE STRUGGLES OF THOSE WHO CAME BEFORE ME.

I COULD SEE MY GRANDPARENTS IN THE KITCHEN WHILE SHE WAS PREPARING OCTOPUS: COULD TASTE THE SEASONINGS AND THE LOVE POURED INTO THE MEAL. I IMAGINED MY GRANDFATHER AS A LARGER THAN LIFE WAR HERO. I FELT LIKE I WAS RIGHT THERE IN JAPAN WHEN MY HE WAS CAPTURED. SHE SAID HE WAS TIED UP AND ESCAPED BY SWIMMING ALL THE WAY BACK TO THE PHILIPPINES. OF COURSE THERE WAS A BIT OF EMBELLISHMENT. BUT LATER WHEN I DECIDED TO SEARCH FOR MY LONG LOST FILIPINO FAMILY, I HAD TO USE THE WORDS AND DOCUMENTATION OF MY GRANDMOTHER TO RE-TRACE THE STEPS OF HIS LIFE. ALL I HAD TO BEGIN THE SEARCH WAS HIS PICTURE AND MY GRANDMOTHER'S STORIES.

BISAYA HATERATION

The idea of locating my long lost family made me become enthusiastic about exploring my roots and connecting with fellow Filipinos. My grandmother's love for Zamboanga instilled in me a deep appreciation for Mindanao, and I often found myself proudly sharing the strong Zamboanga pride when meeting Filipinos. It was the first time I discussed Filipino identity outside of the family setting.

I quickly experienced a profound sense of shame as I watched people's faces contort in disapproval when I mentioned Zamboanga. I only knew the beautiful stories of Mindanao but it seemed so many others likened Zamboanga to the "Wild West" of the Philippines, rife with instability and rebellion. I also noticed the ways the term "Bisaya" was used as an insult. Despite my limited knowledge of the region's history and culture, I sensed the negative connotation.

I was lost and began to feel ashamed of Zamboanga - a feeling I never had until I decided to reclaim my identity and view the rebellion as a symbol of strength. From then on, I represented Mindanao strongly in my music and film and declared myself a warrior.

SHORTLY AFTER THE BURST OF PRIDE, I LOCATED MY LONG LOST FAMILY AND FOUND OUT MY ROOTS WERE ACTUALLY IN MANILA. LEARNING THAT MY GRANDFATHER HAILED FROM BATANGAS AND NOT ZAMBOANGA LEFT ME CONFUSED AND I LET GO OF THE MINDANAO PRIDE AND SLOWLY EMBRACED MY NEWLY FOUND TAGALOG ROOTS.

AFTER IDENTIFYING AS TAGALOG, I STARTED DREAMING OF STINGRAYS AND MANTA RAYS. DELVING INTO DREAM DICTIONARIES SUGGESTED THAT THESE CREATURES SYMBOLIZE GRACE, ELEGANCE, AND FREEDOM, SEEMINGLY RESOLVING THE ENIGMA. HOWEVER, AS THE RAYS CONTINUED TO MULTIPLY AND ALMOST HAUNT ME IN MY DREAMS, I HAD TO KEEP SEARCHING. FINALLY, AN ANSWER EMERGED, AND I UNDERSTOOD THE UNDENIABLE CONNECTION.

A QUARREL ENSUED – EVERYONE WAS BLAMING EACH OTHER.

THE CHIEF SENT THE TOP SWIMMER DOWN BELOW THE BOAT AND TO THE FLOOR OF THE OCEAN TO SEE THE PROBLEM. THEY WERE AMONG THE BEST SWIMMERS IN THE WORLD.

IT TURNS OUT THAT INSTEAD OF STICKING THE POLE DEEP INTO THE SAND, THE POLE GOT LODGED INTO THE MOUTH OF A STINGRAY AND IT PULLED THEM TO THE MIDDLE OF THE OCEAN.

THE SENIOR PRIEST WAS SUMMONED. HE CONSULTED THE DIWATA AND THE VILLAGERS WERE TOLD THAT BEING IN THE MIDDLE OF THE OCEAN WAS A GOOD OMEN.

THEY WERE TOLD TO TRAVEL EAST FOR TWO DAYS AND THEY WOULD ARRIVE AT THEIR DESTINED LOCATION.

THEY FOLLOWED THE STINGRAY FOR TWO DAYS SAILING EAST.

UPON ARRIVAL, THEY TOOK THE POLE, CALLED A SAMBOANG, OUT OF THE MOUTH OF THE STINGRAY AND DUG IT DEEP INTO THE SAND.

THEY NAMED THIS LAND SAMBOANGAN - MOORING PLACE BECAUSE THAT IS WHERE THEY ANCHORED THE POLE INTO THE SAND.

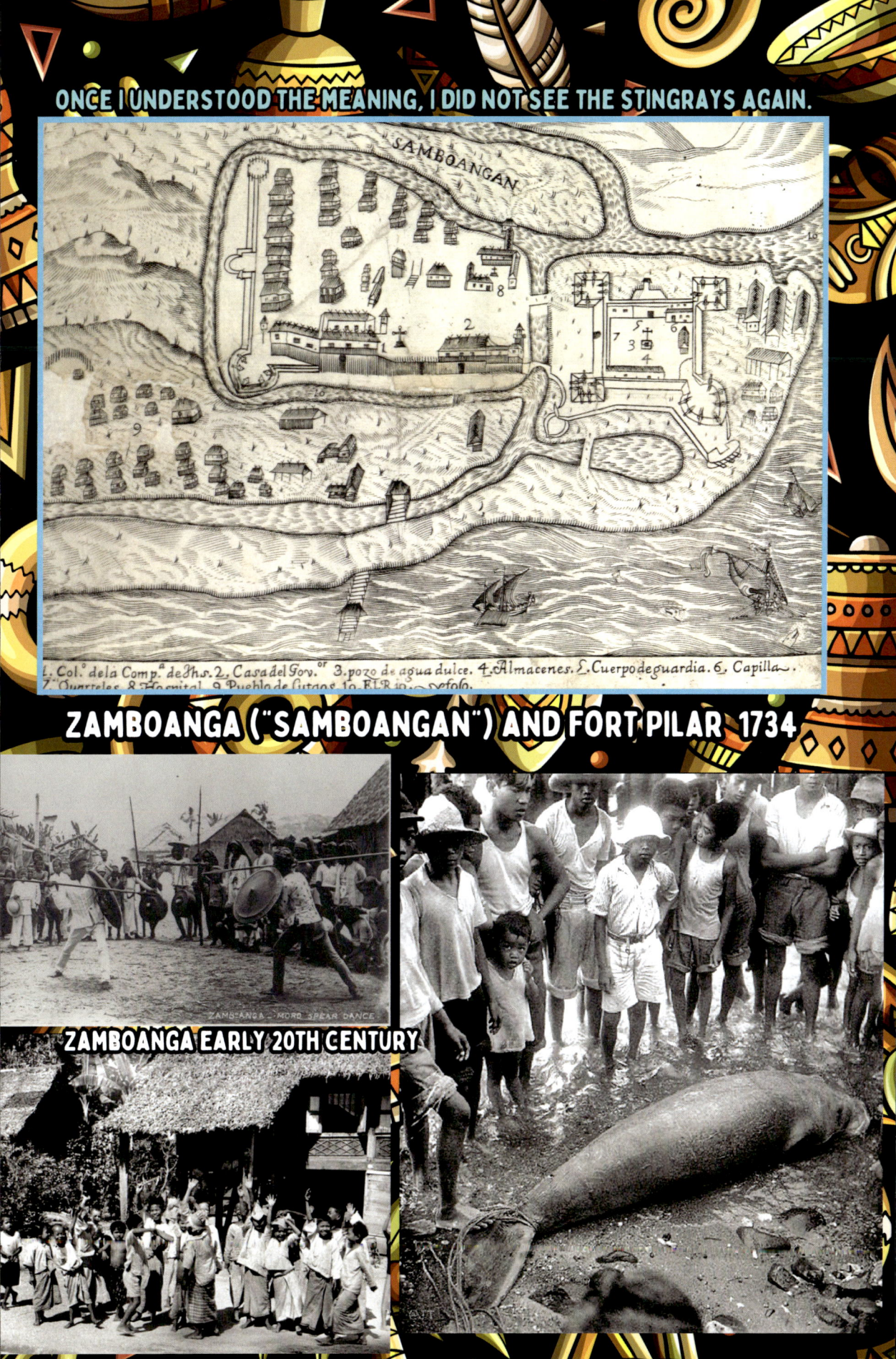

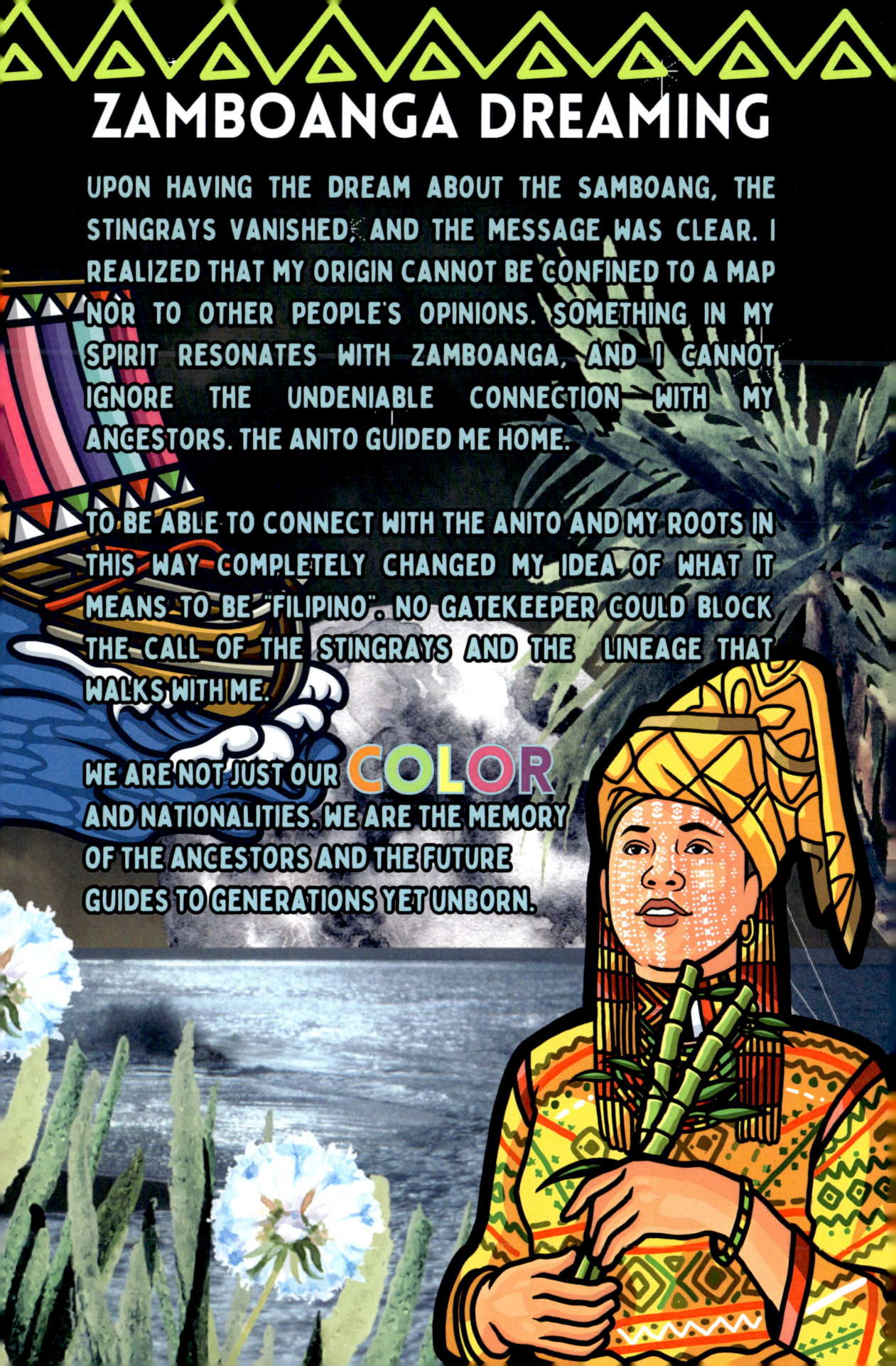

ZAMBOANGA DREAMING

Upon having the dream about the Samboang, the stingrays vanished, and the message was clear. I realized that my origin cannot be confined to a map nor to other people's opinions. Something in my spirit resonates with Zamboanga, and I cannot ignore the undeniable connection with my ancestors. The Anito guided me home.

To be able to connect with the Anito and my roots in this way completely changed my idea of what it means to be "Filipino". No gatekeeper could block the call of the stingrays and the lineage that walks with me.

We are not just our COLOR and nationalities. We are the memory of the ancestors and the future guides to generations yet unborn.

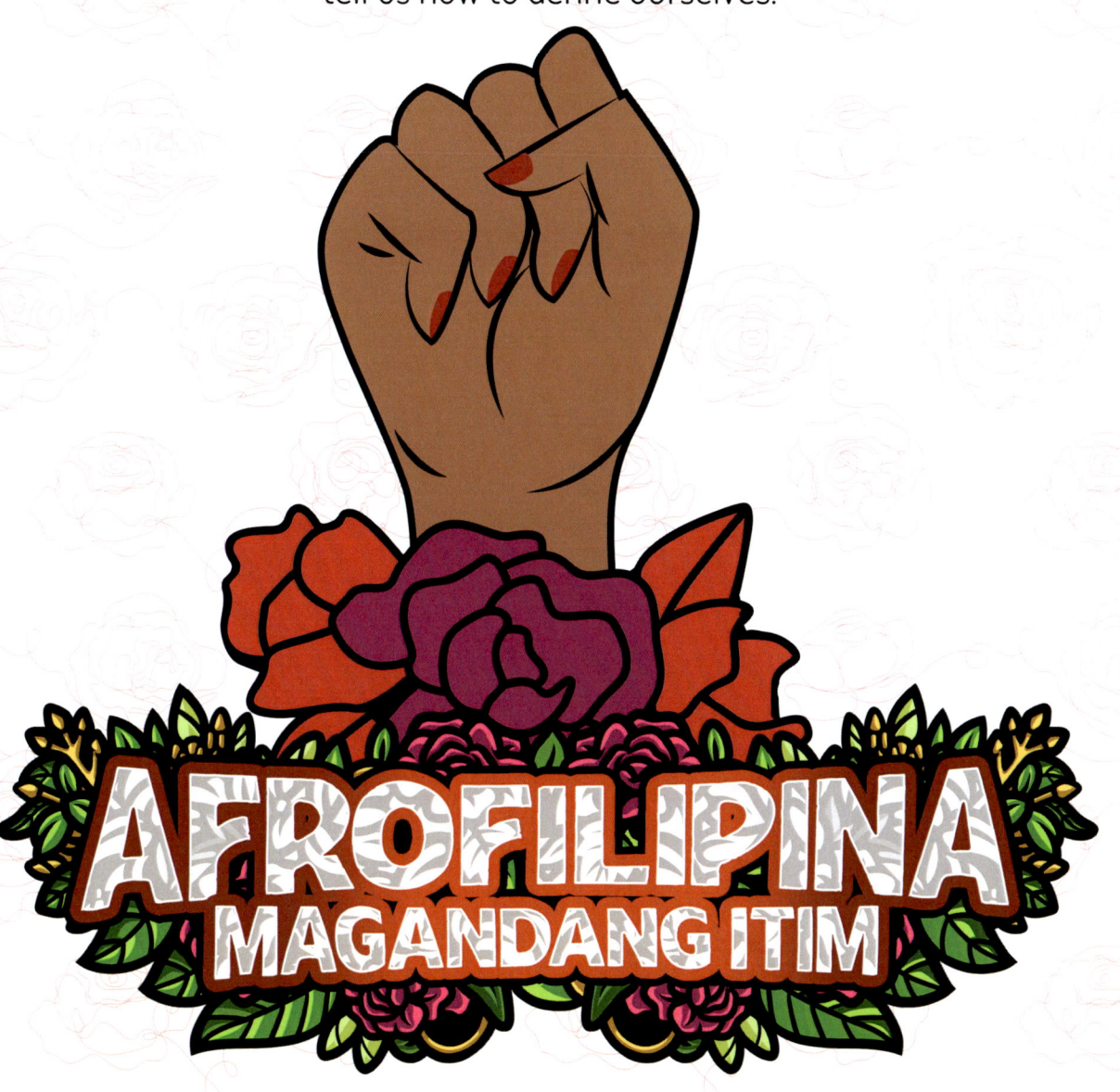

WE DO NOT OWE ANY EXPLANATION OR APOLOGY.
WE DO NOT HAVE TO SHRINK OURSELVES.
WE DO NOT HAVE TO ACCEPT MEAN SPIRITEDNESS.
WE DO NOT HAVE TO ENGAGE THOSE SPACES.
WE DO NOT HAVE TO OPEN OUR SPIRITS TO THEM.
WE DO NOT HAVE TO LISTEN TO THE INSULTS.
WE DO NOT HAVE TO IMPRESS THEM.
WE DO NOT HAVE TO PROVE OURSELF TO ANYONE.
WE DO NOT HAVE TO CHOOSE ONE IDENTITY.
WE DO NOT HAVE TO CHOOSE ONE RACE.
WE DO NOT HAVE TO CHOOSE ONE PARENT.
WE DO NOT HAVE TO CHOOSE ONE CULTURE.
WE DO NOT HAVE TO CHOOSE ONE SIDE.
WE DO NOT HAVE TO ERASE OURSELF.
WE DO NOT HAVE TO PRETEND.
WE DO NOT HAVE TO STAY QUIET.
WE DO NOT HAVE TO SHOW THEM PICTURES.
WE DO NOT HAVE TO LIKE THE FOOD.
WE DO NOT HAVE TO SPEAK THE PERFECT LANGUAGE.
WE DO NOT HAVE TO STRAIGHTEN OUR HAIR.
WE DO NOT HAVE TO STAY OUT OF THE SUN.
WE DO NOT HAVE TO HIDE OUR ROOTS.
WE DO NOT HAVE TO HIDE OUR ROOTS.
WE DO NOT HAVE TO HIDE OUR ROOTS.
WE DO NOT HAVE TO HIDE OUR ROOTS.
WE DO NOT HAVE TO HIDE OUR ROOTS.
WE DO NOT HAVE TO HIDE OUR ROOTS.
WE DO NOT HAVE TO HIDE OUR ROOTS.

MAGANDANG MORENX

I begin this section acknowledging the movement that preceded my own. I want to acknowledge the important work of Asia Jackson and the power of her work to uplift the voices that need uplifting. She continues to be an important beacon using her platform to bring light to the issues of race and colorism in the Philippines and in the diaspora. She started the hashtag #MagandangMorenx in 2016. On her website she states:

> #MagandangMorenx, which translates to "beautiful brown skin," is a powerful movement that confronts the deeply ingrained beauty standards perpetuated by mainstream Filipino media and combats colorism within the culture. From the influence of whitening creams to an entertainment industry saturated with mestizas, the enduring legacy of Spanish colonization has left its mark with the prevalent desire for lighter skin.

https://www.asiajackson.com/magandang-morenx

This movement has been so empowering and significant because colorism is still an unfortunate result of coloniality that persists. People are still using whitening products, pinching noses and holding umbrellas in the sun while telling people to stay out of the sun so they don't get ITIM - black (dark). I am glad Magandang Morenx exists because it is needed and essential. Asia Jackson blazed a trail at a time when no one was speaking out and uplifting the way she has.

AT THE SAME TIME, THERE IS A GAP IN REPRESENTATION. WHO WILL ADVOCATE FOR PEOPLE WHO ARE ITIM - NOT JUST MORENX???

This is why I say

MAGANDANG ITIM

At the time of writing this - **NOBODY** - has joined me in this idea. My phrase has not caught on and as a matter of fact, most people **hate** it. Whenever people hear the phrase they cringe. People love my logo until they look at the bottom of the artwork and see the words **MAGANDANG ITIM**. Plus, with the similarity of the phrases #MagandangItim and #MagandangMorenx, it can appear to be derivative, but it is not. Despite the similarities, they are **NOT** the same. I have to address what is missing for people **who look like ME** and are still **invisibilized** beyond the hashtag #Magandang Morenx .

It is not easy to deal with people dismissing the idea and the way they react, but I am made for this struggle. I am at home in the turbulent volcano and as I walk through lava and keep walking, I am intrigued by every explosion, every eruption, and even the glowing lights I see. Volcanoes erupting is just another part of nature. Though it is one of the most volatile spaces to inhabit, I am content in knowing that the more I face the fire, the more the pressure is relieved for the rest of those who will inherit this fiery mountain.

MORENA? ITIM?

What's the difference? Why can't you just support the other movement without doing something different?

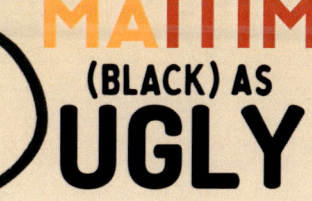

THIS FEED IS FROM QUORA WHERE A PERSON DEFINES **MAITIM (BLACK)** AS **UGLY**

A QUICK SEARCH OF MORENA ON GOOGLE RESULTS IN THE PICTURES OF THE BEAUTIFUL PEOPLE YOU SEE IN THE PHOTO TO THE LEFT. I AM CHEERING THEM ON.

BUT

DO I FIT IN THERE? DO I BLEND IN? AM I REPRESENTED THERE? MY SKIN IS **MORENA** BUT MY FEATURES ARE CLEARLY BLACK.

THEN AGAIN I'M MIXED

WHAT ABOUT THESE PEOPLE?
ARE THEY REPRESENTED WHEN WE UPLIFT MORENA?

MAITIM
(BLACK) IS
UGLY

On Tiktok people are making videos with the above caption stating that MORENA is not BLACK - it is the true color of the beautiful Filipina girl

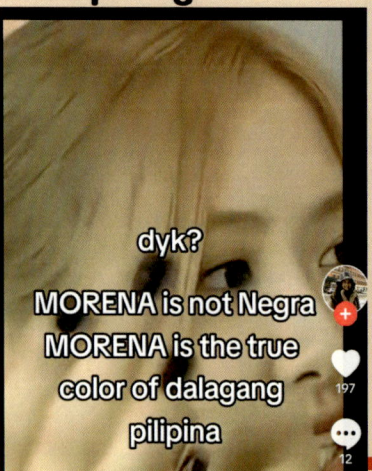

PURE?!?
There is also a movement where people are talking about Filipino races, but BLACK is erased, like Black people do not exist in the Philippines

ITIM

There is no widespread advocacy for the visibility of the ITIM/MAITIM people. No wonder people scoff at my slogan MAGANDANG ITIM - because people really believe that to be BLACK is to be UGLY. We are beyond erased, Itim people are treated terribly and are non-existant in the mainstream culture, opportunities, and educational systems.

People would rather play blackface in a film than to hire an actual Black Filipino. I have heard the arguement that maybe they cannot find the talent among Black Filipinos but with 7,000 islands and over 104 ethnic groups it is hard to believe there is not one talented Black human in the Philippines. This is why I will keep saying

MAGANDANGITIM

Black is not ugly - Black is beautiful - Black is Filipino too and we have to keep saying it until the negative connotation is reversed. People should not be ashamed to be proud to be Black. **BLACK IS NOT UGLY.** Hindi **PANGIT** ay **MAITIM.** WE are NOT UGLY. **BLACK IS BEAUTIUFL!** Magandang ITIM!

BLACK IS NOT UGLY. HINDI PANGIT AY MAITIM. WE ARE NOT UGLY. BLACK IS BEAUTIUFL! MAGANDANG ITIM!

SO WHO IS AFROFILIPINA?

When I was younger, I thought AfroFilipina meant Black and Filipino mixed – as in African American or AfroCaribbean etc. and Filipino. However, through time, my definition has expanded to include ANYONE who is ITIM (Black) or preseumed to be ITIM with roots in the Philippine Islands.

In my definition of AfroFilipina, this includes morena Filipina/o/x people who have curly hair and dark skin, Indigenous Black people, and people who are mixed with Filipino and other people of the African diaspora.

If you look Black or are percieved to be BLACK you are treated Maitim – Black and UGLY, I created this work for you. I do not agree with our identity being ugly but that is the way we are made to feel. In my experience, so many moreno (Brown) people have been racist towards me for being Black. We need a hashtag too, we need a movement too! Who is fighting and rewriting the story? It has to be us!

WE NEED HEALING

HURT PEOPLE HURT PEOPLE

LET'S LOOK DEEPER
🔍 BLACK PEOPLE OF ASIA

The term **NEGRITO** has been used interchangeably with **AETA** to refer to dark-skinned indigenous people of the Philippines.

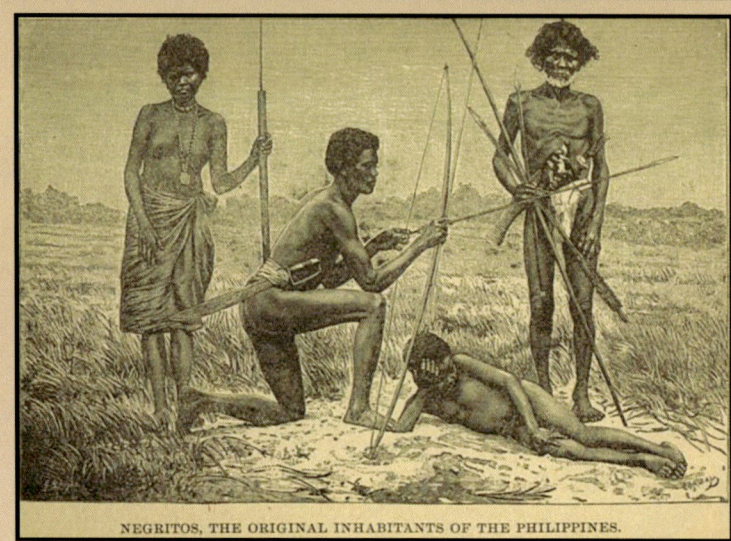

NEGRITOS, THE ORIGINAL INHABITANTS OF THE PHILIPPINES.

However, it is important to recognize that Negritos and Aetas are not a monolithic group, and Negritos can be found beyond the Philippines. The term "Negrito" originated from the Spanish colonizers to describe the dark-skinned indigenous people of the Philippines. Over time, other European groups adopted the term to refer to various groups of people who share similar physical characteristics, such as relatively small physical stature and dark skin. This includes the Pygmies of Central Africa.

The Negrito population can be found throughout Southeast Asia and the Andaman Islands, including the Andamanese peoples, the Great Andamanese, the Onge, the Jarawa, and the Sentinelese. Additionally, Negritos can be found among the Semang peoples, the Batek people of Peninsular Malaysia, the Maniq people of Southern Thailand, and the Aeta of Luzon, the Ati and Tumandok of Panay, the Mamanwa of Mindanao, and approximately 30 other officially recognized ethnic groups in the Philippines.

NEGRITO PEOPLES

ANDAMESE OF INDIA

BATEK PEOPLE OF MALAYSIA

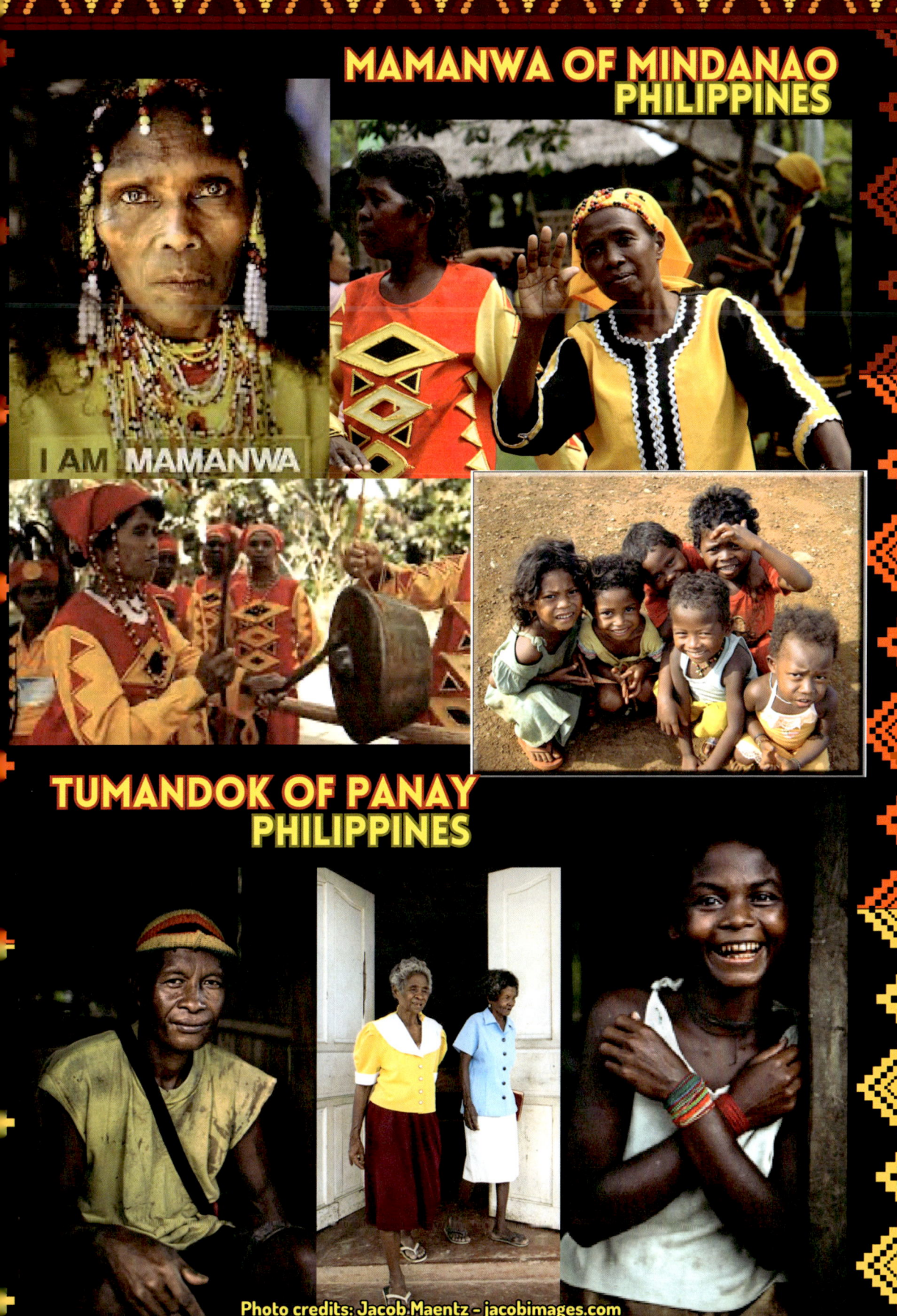

TYPES OF NEGRITOS IN THE PHILIPPINE ISLANDS[1]

By ROBERT BENNETT BEAN

THE Aetas, or Negritos, of the Philippines have been studied at close range by Meyer, Montano, Reed, and others, and from a distance by many anthropologists. The Honorable Dean C. Worcester, Secretary of the Interior of the Philippine Islands, has visited the Negritos wherever in the archipelago they could be found; yet never before have they been classified into types, although at least three types are represented among them — three types that are the fundamental units of mankind — the Primitive, the Iberian, and the Australoid. The most plausible supposition to account for the three types among the Negritos is that the Australoid preceded the Iberian and Primitive, who have been incorporated with the Australoid as the result of recent or remote intrusions. By the workings of Mendelian heredity the kinky hair, black skin, and diminutive stature of the Australoid have obscured the characteristics of the other types.

This is the first study dealing with the ears and physical characteristics of the Philippine Islanders of the interior and is based largely on photographs in the collection of the Bureau of Science of the Philippine Government, and in the private collection of Mr. Worcester, to whom I am indebted for access to both collections.

The Negritos are the first of the inland tribes selected for study, because they are relatively few in number and are undoubtedly becoming fewer, as they lose their purity when they come into contact with surrounding peoples. They were selected also because very few studies of Negritos have been made dealing with the physical characteristics of the living, and no previous study has been made of their ears; and, finally, because a large number of representative

---

[1] The photographs of the Negritos in this paper are reproduced with the permission of the Secretary of the Interior of the Philippine Islands and the editor of the Philippine Journal of Science, in which journal they were originally published.

AETA

below is a list of just some of the subgroups of the Aeta

- **AETA – CENTRAL LUZON**
  - Ambala Aeta – Zambales, Bataan
  - Abellen Aeta (also Abenlen, Abelling or Aburlin) – Tarlac
  - Magbukún Aeta (also Magbikin, Magbeken, or Bataan Ayta) – Bataan
  - Mag-antsi Aeta (also Mag-anchi or Magganchi) – Zambales, Tarlac, Pampanga
  - Mag-indi Aeta (also Maggindi) – Zambales, Pampanga

- **AGTA – SOUTHEASTERN LUZON**
  - Alabat Agta (also Alabat Island Agta) – Quezon
  - Agta Cimarron – Camarines Sur
  - Manide (also Abiyan Agta or Camarines Norte Agta) – Camarines Norte
  - Rinconada Agta (also Iriga Agta) – Camarines Sur
  - Tabangnon (also Partido Agta, Katabangan, Katubung, or Isarog Agta) – Sorsogon, Quezon, Camarines Sur

- **DUMAGAT – EASTERN LUZON**
  - Alta
  - Northern Alta – Aurora
  - Southern Alta (also Kabulowan Alta or Edimala) – Quezon, Nueva Ecija
  - Arta – Quirino
  - Atta
  - Faire-Rizal Atta – Cagayan province
  - Pamplona Atta – Cagayan province
  - Pudtol Atta – Cagayan province
  - Casiguran Dumagat – Aurora
  - Central Cagayan Dumagat – Cagayan
  - Palanan Dumagat – Isabela
  - Paranan Dumagat (or Pahanan Dumagat) – Isabela
  - Disabungan Dumagat – Isabela
  - Dupaningan Dumagat – Cagayan
  - Madella Dumagat – Quirino
  - Sinauna Tagalog (also Remontado Dumagat) – Rizal, Quezon
  - Umiray Dumagat – Quezon

Dumagat

Alabat

Ambala

A NOTE ABOUT INDIGENOUS PEOPLES

For centuries, Indigenous peoples have been idealized and objectified. They are often fetishized for their ancient practices, profound understanding of the earth and herbs, as well as their spiritual mystique. Yet beneath the "admiration" lies condescendance (primative), erasure, and the threat of extinction beause many Indigenous peoples are being chased from their homelands, massacred, and forced into exile, especially many of the Black Indigenous groups named on the prior pages.

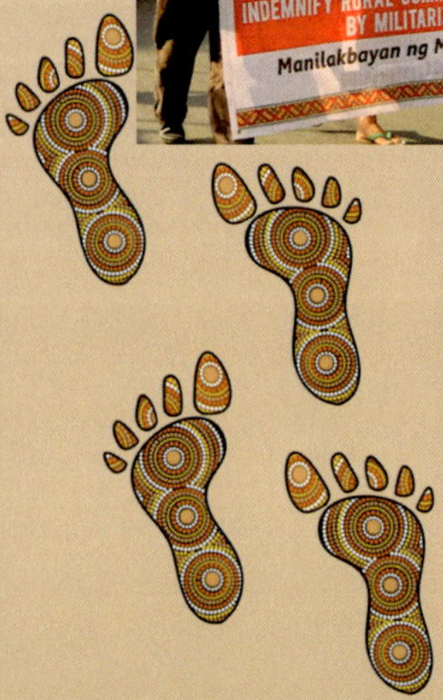

IT'S DEEPER THAN THE SKIN

If only we all could experience the world through the lens of those who love us the most. We would always be beautiful.

There were no mirrors in my Nana's house,
no mirrors in my Nana's house.
There were no mirrors in my Nana's house,
no mirrors in my Nana's house.
And the beauty that I saw in everything
was in her eyes (like the rising of the sun).

I never knew that my skin was too black.
I never knew that my nose was too flat.
I never knew that my clothes didn't fit.
I never knew there were things that I'd missed,
cause the beauty in everything
was in her eyes (like the rising of the sun);
...was in her eyes.

-- By Ysaye Maria Barnwell
(1992)

The world is NOT our Nana's house. A bigger colonial agenda has sought to convince people of color all over the world that who and what they are, is inferior to those who have colonized them. This is echoed in the mainstream media and the symbolic images that represent the people. Filipinos are not exempt, as you will see on the pages that follow.

CASTAS EXISTED IN THE PHILIPPINES
The Spaniards created caste systems of racial stratification in their colonial systems.

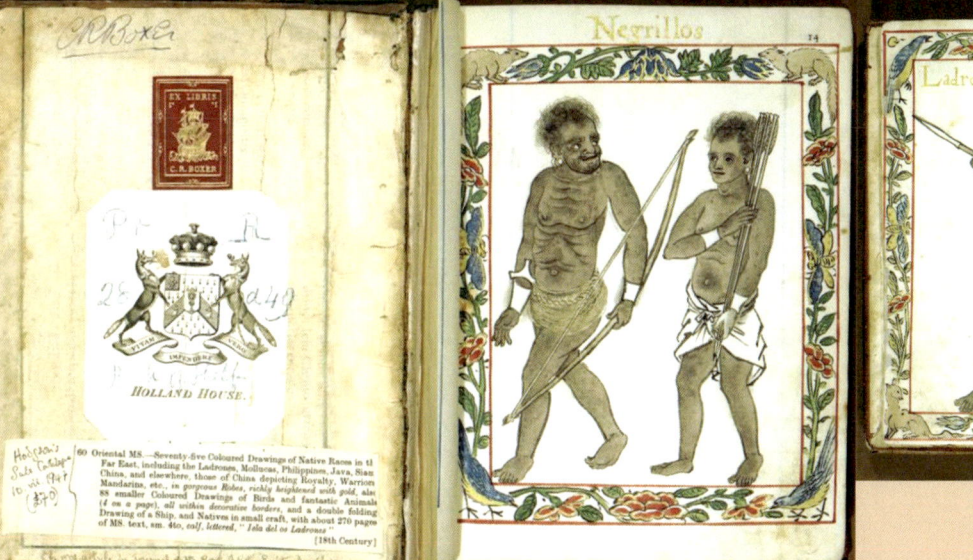

THERE WAS AN ATTEMPT TO RELOCATE U.S. BLACK PEOPLE TO THE PHILIPPINES.

NEGROES TO THE PHILIPPINES.

Senator Morgan's Scheme of Civilization.

HIS PLAN WILL BE INVESTIGATED BY PRESIDENT ROOSEVELT AND HIS CABINET.

Washington, Dec. 15—Senator John T Morgan, of Alabama, has succeeded, after two years of endeavor in interesting the war department and incidentally President Roosevelt in a plan to use the Philippine Islands in colonizing the Negroes of the United States.

The war department has made arrangements to test the practical possibilities of a plan and the president sent a special envoy, T. Thomas Fortune, a Negro leader to the Philippine Islands to make investigations and report on the conditions there.

In his efforts to have the plan put in execution, Senator Morgan has held frequent consultations with Secretary of War, Root; has consulted Govenor-General, Taft, and in other ways urged his scheme on the officials.

It is the Alabama Senator's purpose in the future to start legislation in congress for the movement to colonize the Negroes in the Philippines. He has not pushed this part of his work because he believes the time is not ripe yet for the legislation; the farmers of the south, he says, think they need the Negro now, and until conditions are more favorable, he will with hold the proposed legislation. He believes, however, that the move now under way will result eventually in millions of the Negroes emigrating to the Philippine Islands and working out their own salvation.

This, he says is the solution of the grave Negro question which confronts the American people.

Senator Morgan's plan is to incorporate for the Negroes, steamship transportation companies; to give to them homestead of about twenty acres each in the island and to give them the best possible commercial advantage. The plan would not deprive them of their protection under the flag of the United States; it would not deprive them of citizenship, of which they are proud, and it would enable them to become a self-sustaining and prosperous race of people, because the land in the Philippine Island is extremely rich and fertile. The climate is exactly suited to the Negroes physical and industrial character.—Ex.

"Negroes to the Philippines," The Informer, February 1903. Courtesy of The Ohio Historical Society

Sen. John T. Morgan - Alabama

T. Thomas Fortune (October 3, 1856 – June 2, 1928) was an American orator, civil rights leader, journalist, writer, editor and publisher. He was a long-time adviser to Booker T. Washington and was the editor of Washington's first autobiography. Fortune's philosophy of militant agitation on behalf of the rights of Black people laid one of the foundations of the Civil Rights Movement. Timothy Thomas Fortune was born into slavery in Marianna, Jackson County, Florida

SPANISH-AMERICAN WAR

Similar images to those that were utilized to stereotype African Americans were also used to depict Filipinos to justify their discriminatory actions and attitudes towards Filipinos.

FILIPINOS AS BARBARIC AND IN NEED OF CIVILIZATION

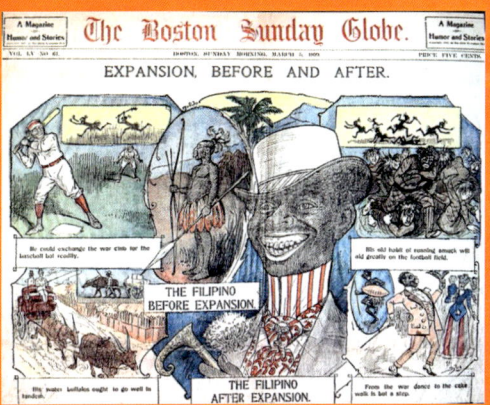

Boston Sunday Globe (1899), It is important to note that 1899 is the beginning of the Philippine-American War (1899-1902).

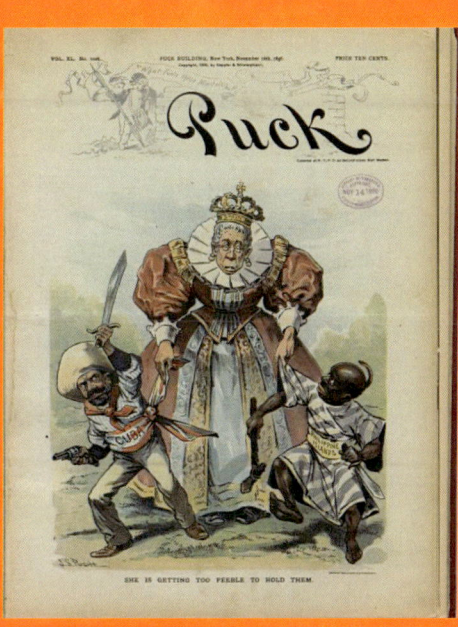

A woman with a crown reading "Spain", looks like she's carrying out two indisciplined children. On the left is a man with "Cuba" on his shirt. He carries a sword raised high in the air in one hand and a gun in the other. sword, and the other labeled "Philippine Islands", he carries what looks like an indigenous hatchet and a knife in the other hand. The caption reads, "She is getting too Feeble to hold them". via Puck Building 1896.

Notice the belt sashes of the students in the front saying (L to R) Philipines, Hawaii, Porto Rico and Cuba. Also do you notice the Black man in the far left corner cleaning the windows but not permitted to study. There are so many details to study in this photo from 1899.
The text at the bottom of the image reads:
Uncle Sam (to his new class in Civilization): Now, children, you've got to learn these lessons whether you want to or not! But just take a look at the class ahead of you, and remember that, in a little while, you will feel as glad to be here as they are!

SPANISH-AMERICAN WAR

Following its defeat in the Spanish-American War of 1898, Spain relinquished its long-held territory, the Philippines, to the United States in the Treaty of Paris. However, just two days before U.S. Senate ratified the treaty, fighting erupted between American forces and Filipino nationalists led by Emilio Aguinaldo, who wanted independence rather than a change in colonial rulers. This conflict, known as the Philippine-American War, spanned three years and resulted in the deaths of over 4,200 American and 20,000 Filipino combatants. Tragically, as many as 200,000 Filipino civilians lost their lives due to violence, famine, and disease.

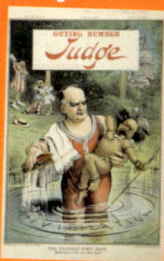

HUMAN ZOOS
LIVING EXHIBITS AT 1904 WORLD FAIR

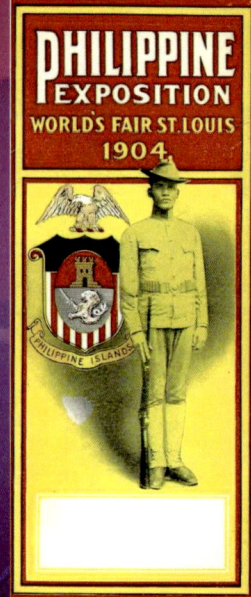

Black and Asian people were put on display in "Human Zoos" from 1904 to as late as 1958. In 1904 after the Spanish-American war when they acquired Puerto Rico, Guam and the Philippines, they decided to put the native people on "display". The St. Louis World Fair Exhibit of humans was in conjunction with the 1904 Summer Olympics.

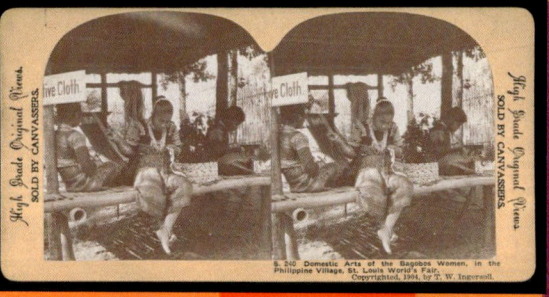

Title:
Moro Family in the Philippine Village exhibit in the Department of Anthropology at the 1904 World's Fair.
1904 Source: Missouri History Museum

INDIGENOUS AETAS POSING AT THE ST. LOUIS WORLD'S FAIR
(with the "missing link" shown second from the right).

[From "Philippine Exposition: World's Fair St. Louis 1904," brochure, edited by Alfred C. Newell, 1904]

WATSONVILLE RIOTS

During a span of five days from January 19 to 23, 1930, Watsonville, California, was the scene of racial violence. Filipino American farm workers were subjected to violent attacks by white residents who were against immigration. These riots exposed the racial and socioeconomic tensions that existed in California's agricultural communities.

THE RIOTS STARTED BECAUSE THE FILIPINOS IN A CLUB DANCED WITH WHITE WOMEN

WHITE MOBS THREW FILIPINOS OFF OF THE PAJARO RIVER BRIDGE IN WATSONVILLE

1930 In the aftermath of a chain or riots following Watsonville. There was devastating bombing of Taxi Dance Club a Filipino club - bombed by white rioters in Stockton. Source: Filipino American National Historical Society

FERMIN TOBERA
His name should never be forgotten.

Fermin Tobera died at age 22 after being shot in the heart when he was hiding in a closet with 11 others, trying to avoid the rounds of bullets fired at a bunkhouse in Murphy Ranch in San Juan Road on January 23. The body of Fermin Tobera was sent home to the Philippines. He is considered a martyr, a symbol of the Filipinos' fight for independence and equality.

BLACKFACE PERSISTS IN THE PHILIPPINES

Nita Negrita 2011

The series, beginning in 2011 only lasted one season and was contested by German professor Axel Honneth who contended with the correlation of Blackness with poverty and also the issue that they presented a caricature of Black people as opposed to the actual culture of the people.

RC COLA COMMERCIAL - 2020

Family drinking off of the back of the young man

In November 2020 RC Cola teamed up with agency Gigil, Taguig to produce a quirky ad that took the Philippines by storm and quickly became part of pop culture. The creative was titled "Nyahahakbkxjbcjhishdishlsab@!!!! Basta RC Cola!" and featured a young boy coming home and revealing to his mother that he was being bullied at school for being adopted.ABtears streaming down his face, the son takes off his backpack to reveal four drinking glasses sprouting from his back The ad concludes with the mother pouring cola from her neck into the glasses and the entire family drinking through straws from the boy's back.

THE IRONY
FILIPINO FILMS DEPICT BLACK PEOPLE IN BLACK FACE. MEANWHILE, SOME OTHER ASIANS DEPICT FILIPINOS IN BLACK FACE.

A controversy sparked when a Chinese actor in Malaysia represented a Filipina character in Blackface. In other words, Filipinos play "Black" characters in blackface, but when other Asians represent Filipinos, this is an example of how Filipinos are percieved by them.

Hong Kong

'Blackface' advert where Chinese man plays Filipina maid sparks race row in Hong Kong

Malaysian bank pulls video featuring Chinese actor playing a Filipino domestic helper

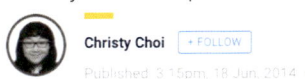

Christy Choi + FOLLOW

Published: 3:15pm, 18 Jun, 2014

Why you can trust SCMP

Hong Leong bank has pulled the ad from its website after it was inundated with complaints. Photo: YouTube

An advertisement for domestic helper insurance starring a Chinese man as a Filipino maid has been withdrawn after it was condemned as racist – but the bank responsible insisted it never intended to cause offence.

WE ARE IN THE SAME BOAT EVEN IF WE DO NOT WANT TO BE

and it's not a bad thing... it's only percieved as bad because of the negative connotation colonizers have attached to Blackness.

Filipinos are often referred to as "The BLACK People of ASIA," and this term carries multiple interpretations. On one hand, it can be a way of endearing Filipinos by acknowledging their cool and edgy style, similar to how the Black culture is perceived. However, on the other hand, it can also be used negatively and intended as an insult to denigrate Filipinos.

Black people from all around the world have suffered from mistreatment and stereotyping. The negative portrayal of these individuals has led many to avoid any association with Blackness, and it seems that people are being punished for simply their proximity to or appearance of Blackness.

I grew up in an environment that told me **BLACK IS BEAUTIFUL** and I believe it! But what if I grew up in a world that taught me that everything about me was ugly?

BEAUTY AND THE BESTIE (2015)
For an important case, a policeman needs the help of his former best friend to impersonate the daughter of a foreign dignitary in a beauty pageant. (ABS-CBN)

As I delved into my Filipino heritage, I began to ponder what it would be like to exist in a world where I was perceived as "pangit." The image above shows a comparison between a still from the movie Beauty and the Bestie (2015) and a photo of myself. In the film, the beauty queen was also labeled as "pangit," but the only difference was her hair, which resembles mine in every way. This raises an important question – what about other Filipinos or indigenous people who share my physical appearance? What kind of message does this sort of media representation send to them?

I finally got my Filipiniana dress and found communities where I was accepted for who I am. I became a model/advocate for MUSA a fashion house from Davao, Philippines that is just as proud of our Mindanao heritage as I am. It gave me great pride that the cloth I wear is from the region of my Ancestors.

As I walked the runway in New York Fashion Week the audience cheered and I had the opportunity to make my debut singing in Tagalog at this major event with MUSA. That event expanded to going on an international tour that took me places like Japan, Las Vegas, and Paris. Things finally came full circle. I realized it wasn't about the dress at all. I discovered that being Filipino is more than just about looks or blood quantum; it's about the strength of my roots, the resilience of my ancestors, and the spirit that they have passed down to me. Their warrior spirit is in my blood, as is their kindness and strength. We do not need anyone's permission to be who we are. Through that understanding, I transformed from a turbulent volcano to a beautiful glowing river of lava.

AFROFILIPINO HISTORY

MARPESSA DAWN

BIRTHPLACE: PITTSBURGH, PENNSYLVANIA USA

BIRTH DATE: JANUARY 3, 1934

DIED: AUGUST 25, 2008 (AGED 74) PARIS, FRANCE

ETHNICITY: FILIPINA-AMERICAN (FRENCH CITIZEN)

PROFESSION: ACTRESS, SINGER, AND DANCER

Marpessa Dawn, who gained worldwide recognition for her portrayal of Euridyce in Black Orpheus, was born in Pennsylvania, PA in 1934. Prior to her move to Europe, she worked as a lab technician in New York. Dawn began her acting career in England, where she landed a few minor TV roles. In 1953, she relocated to France, where she occasionally worked as a governess and performed as a singer and dancer in nightclubs. It was during this time that she met director Marcel Camus, who would cast her as "Eurydice" in his film Black Orpheus at the age of 24.

Black Orpheus won the Palme d'Or at the 1959 Cannes Film Festival and the 1960 Academy Award for Best Foreign Language Film. She was also featured in Ebony Magazine in November 1959. Sadly she and her co-star from the film, Brazilian actor Breno Mello, passed away just 45 days apart in 2008, both from heart attacks.

H.E.R
Gabriella Sarmiento Wilson

BIRTHPLACE: VALLEJO, CALIFORNIA- USA
BIRTH DATE: JUNE 27, 1997
ETHNICITY: FILIPINA-AMERICAN
PROFESSION: SINGER, MUSICIAN, SONGWRITER

H.E.R. is an acronym for "Having Everything Revealed yet there is an air of mystery with the artist known as H.E.R.. From her signature glasses to her beautiful voluminous, wavy locks of hair. H.E.R. is mesmerizing as she plays guitar solos or sings R&B tunes on stage. The multi-talented artist plays 5 instruments including her voice. Beyond music, H.E.R. has also had some success in acting. Recently appearing in the screen adaptation of the musical The Color Purple as the character Squeak and making history playing the role of Belle in Beauty and the Beast. She put Baybayin letters on her apron that spelled out Bel (Belle). She has received an Academy Award, a Children's and Family Emmy Award, and five Grammy Awards, along with nominations for a Golden Globe Award, three American Music Awards, and four Billboard Music Awards.

SUGARPIE DE SANTO
UMPEYLIA MARSEMA BALINTO

BIRTHPLACE: BROOKLYN, NEW YORK - USA
BIRTH DATE: OCTOBER 16, 1935
ETHNICITY: FILIPINA-AMERICAN
PROFESSION: ACTRESS, SINGER, AND DANCER

De Santo was the oldest girl in a family of 10 children who grew up in the Fillmore district. Her Filipino father worked making mattresses. Her African American mother was from Philadelphia. Growing up she was friends with Etta James. Johnny Otis discovered DeSanto in 1955, and she toured with the Johnny Otis Revue. Otis gave her the stage name Sugar Pie. In 1959 and 1960, she toured with the James Brown Revue.

In 1960, DeSanto rose to national prominence when her single "I Want to Know", reached number four on Billboard's Hot R&B chart. DeSanto was married to Pee Wee Kingsley in the 1950s. After that marriage ended, she was married to Jesse Earl Davis for 27 years. In October 2006, Davis died attempting to extinguish a fire that destroyed their apartment in Oakland, California. DeSanto continues to perform and sing today.

ELIZABETH RAMSEY
Queen of Philippine Rock N' Roll

BIRTHPLACE: SAN CARLOS CITY, NEGROS OCCIDENTAL - PHILIPPINES

BIRTH DATE: DECEMBER 3, 1931

DIED: AUGUST 25, 2008 (AGED 74) MANILA, PHILIPPINES

ETHNICITY: FILIPINA-JAMAICAN

PROFESSION: COMEDIENNE, SINGER, ACTRESS, AND QUEEN OF FILIPINO SOUL MUSIC

Elizabeth Ramsey was a Filipina singer, comedian, and actress. During her almost six-decade career, she established herself as an iconic showbiz personality and entertainer. Ramsey's unique appearance courtesy of her Filipino-Jamaican blood, stage antics, irreverent humor, and punchlines delivered in her heavy Visayan accent brought her into prominence in the Filipino entertainment industry. She is also the mother of popular AfroFilipina singer Jaya. Ramsey's career began in 1958 after winning a singing contest in Student Canteen. . Her raspy vocals and energetic live performances of rock and roll songs earned her the title as the Philippine's "Queen of Rock and Roll". In the 1990s, she returned to the Philippines after living in the United States for several years and made a successful comeback by appearing in numerous movies and TV shows. Ramsey died October 8, 2015, in her sleep and a memoir - Elizabeth Ramsey: Queen of Philippine Rock N' Roll (2017) was written by her daughter Sansy Ramsey in her memory.

APL.DE.AP
(ALLAN PINEDA LINDO, JR.)

BIRTHPLACE: ANGELES CITY, PAMPANGA - PHILIPPINES

BIRTH DATE: NOVEMBER 28, 1974

ETHNICITY: FILIPINO-AMERICAN

PROFESSION: SINGER, RAPPER, PRODUCER

Apl.de.Ap is a Filipino American musician, rapper, record producer, entrepreneur & philanthropist who rose to fame as a co-founder/member of the Grammy Award-winning hip hop group The Black Eyed Peas. Outside of creating music, Apl is a regular judge on the hit show, The Voice: Teen, Philippines and is also the founder of the Apl.de.ap Foundation which focuses on supporting youth to grant opportunities through arts, technology and healthcare in the Philippines. His African American father, an airman stationed at Clark Air Base, left the family shortly after his birth; his Filipino mother, raised him as a single mother. The Pearl S. Buck Foundation, an organization that finds healthier living environments for young, abandoned, or orphaned American children, matched him with a sponsor through a dollar-a-day program.

He initially came to the United States at the age of eleven for treatment for nystagmus, an involuntary movement of the eyes. At fourteen he moved permanently to the USA. Aside being fluent in English, Pineda is a native speaker of two Philippine languages: Tagalog and Kapampangan.

RAYMOND TOWNSEND
FIRST FILIPINO IN THE NBA

BIRTHPLACE: SAN JOSE, CALIFORNIA USA
BIRTH DATE: DECEMBER 20, 1955
ETHNICITY: FILIPINO-AMERICAN
PROFESSION: BASKETBALL PLAYER, FORMER NBA

Not only was he the first Filipino in the NBA, but as he states, he remained the only Filipino for at least 35 years. He talks about how he could have been more vocal about who he was, but he realized people had the perception that Filipinos were not supposed to be in the NBA. Townsend was born to a Filipina mother and an African American father. Townsend's brother, Kurtis, is an assistant coach for the Kansas Jayhawks. After his basketball playing career, Townsend worked as youth sports development coordinator in San Jose, California.

JOE BATAAN
BATAAN NITOLLANO

AFROFILIPINO

BIRTHPLACE: SPANISH HARLEM, NEW YORK USA

BIRTH DATE: NOVEMBER 15, 1942

ETHNICITY: FILIPINO-AMERICAN

PROFESSION: MUSICIAN, SINGER, PIANIST

Bataan was influenced by two musical styles: the Latin boogaloo and African American doo-wop. Though Bataan was neither the first nor only artist to combine doo-wop-style singing with Latin rhythms, his talent for it drew the attention of Fania Records. In 1973, he helped coin the phrase "salsoul", lending its name to his first post-Fania album. In early 2009, Bataan was featured in the Kenzo Digital-produced "beat cinematic" City of God's Son. Bataan was featured as the narrator of the story, playing the part of an older Nas reflecting upon his youth in the street with cohorts Jay-Z, Ghostface Killah, Biggie and Raekwon. Bataan continues to leave his mark on the world through music and community.

NORMAN KING
THE FIRST AETA TO GRADUATE FROM A TOP PHILIPPINES UNIVERSITY

BIRTHPLACE: PORAC PAMPANGA, LUZON - PHILIPPINES

BIRTH DATE: (DAY UNKNOWN) 1989

ETHNICITY: AETA

PROFESSION: SCHOLAR, FUTURE LAWYER

"Dapat laging magkaisa."
(we must always be united)
Words of wisdom from Norman King's mother, Warlita King

The story of Norman King is so inspirational they made it into a beautiful short film in 2018 – "Safeguard: Pabaon sa Buhay". This film featured actual Aeta actors playing the role of Aetas as well. This is significant, because as mentioned before, some films in the Philppines use blackface instead of hiring Aeta actors.

As a young Indigenous boy, King experienced the typical roadblocks to success. Skin color, economic constraints, and native heritage subjected him to bouts with bullying as he was growing up. Empowered by the wisdom of his mother, he worked hard and funded his college education. In Manila, he found solidarity in a supportive community at the University of the Philippines, where he earned his Bachelor of Arts degree in Behavioral Science in 2017. After graduating, he returned to Pampanga serving the Aeta community, while raising public awareness about their issues.

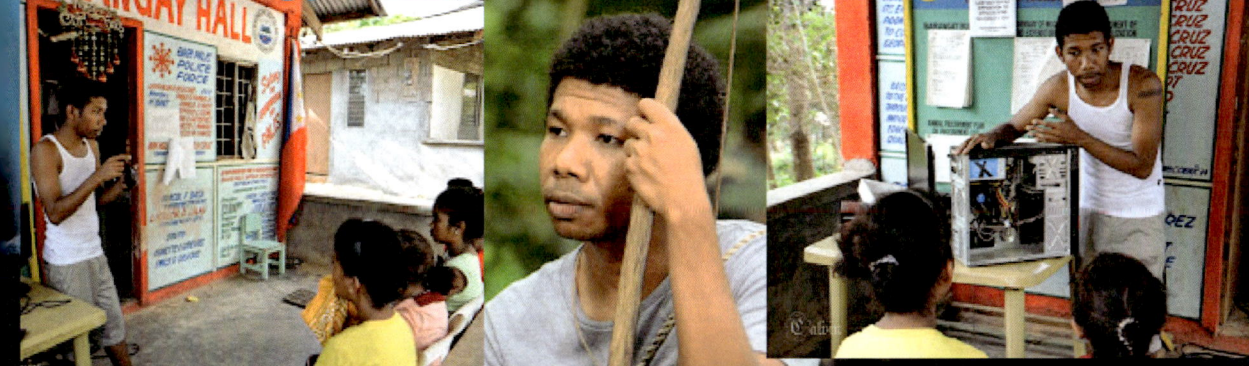

DAVID FAGEN

BIRTHPLACE: TAMPA, FLORIDA - USA

BIRTH DATE: UNKNOWN 1875

DIED: UNKNOWN - PHILIPPINES
ETHNICITY: AFRICAN AMERICAN

PROFESSION: SOLDIER (PHILIPPINE AMERICAN WAR)/ PHILIPPINES REVOLUTION - BUFFALO SOLDIER

In 1899, during a campaign on the island of Luzon to entrap the Filipino revolutionary president Emilio Aguinaldo, a 21-year-old Buffalo Soldier named David Fagen deserted from the American army.

His defection was likely a reaction to racist treatment of African-American soldiers within the United States armed forces at the time, as well as racist sentiments expressed towards the Filipino resistance, who were frequently referred to by American soldiers by the "n" word and as "gugus". As the war ended, the US gave amnesties to most of their opponents. A substantial reward was offered for Fagen, who was considered a traitor. There are two conflicting versions of his fate: one is that his was the partially decomposed head for which the reward was claimed, and the other is that he married a local woman and lived peacefully in the mountains.

THURGOOD & CECILIA MARSHALL

WHEN SUPREME COURT JUSTICE THURGOOD MARSHALL TOOK HIS SEAT AT THE COURT FOR THE FIRST TIME ON OCT. 2, 1967, HIS FAMILY WAS ON HAND TO WATCH. THE JUSTICE WAS JOINED BY HIS WIFE, CECILIA "CISSY" MARSHALL, AND TWO SONS, THURGOOD JR. AND JOHN. (HENRY GRIFFIN/AP)

CREDIT: (SARAH L. VOISIN/THE WASHINGTON POST)

Thurgood Marshall Jr. (L) and John W. Marshall (R) are the sons of Justice Thurgood Marshall. He was the first Black American to serve on the U.S. Supreme Court and Cecilia Suyat Marshall, a Filipina American was a civil rights activist and historian from Hawaii . She spent her life preserving history and continued to fight for civil rights. Marshall Jr. is a Lawyer who served as chairman of the Board of Governors of the United States Postal Service and John W. Marshall is a a former Virginia Secretary of Public Safety and former U.S. Marshals Service Director.

DEXTER SANTOS VALENTON
FIRST AETA TO PASS CRIMINOLOGY LICENSURE EXAM

BIRTHPLACE: FLORIDABLANCA TOWN, PAMPANGA - PHILIPPINES

BIRTH DATE: 2000

ETHNICITY: AETA, INDIGINEOUS FILIPINO

PROFESSION: LICENSED CRIMINOLOGIST AND FUTURE OFFICER

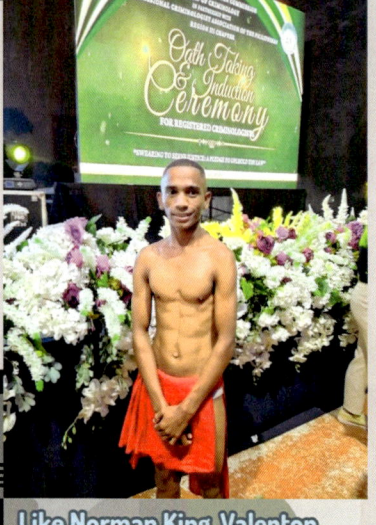

Like Norman King, Valenton also attended graduation in the Aeta traditional attire.

Dexter Santos Valenton made history at age 23 in 2023 by being the first known Aeta to pass the state's criminologist licensure test of the Professional Regulation Commission. Not only did he pass, but he did so with flying colors. Valenton's achievement paves the way for other members of indigenous communities. If he joins the local police force he will also make history as the first member of the indigenous community to be part of the police force.

JUSTIN BAUTISTA JONES

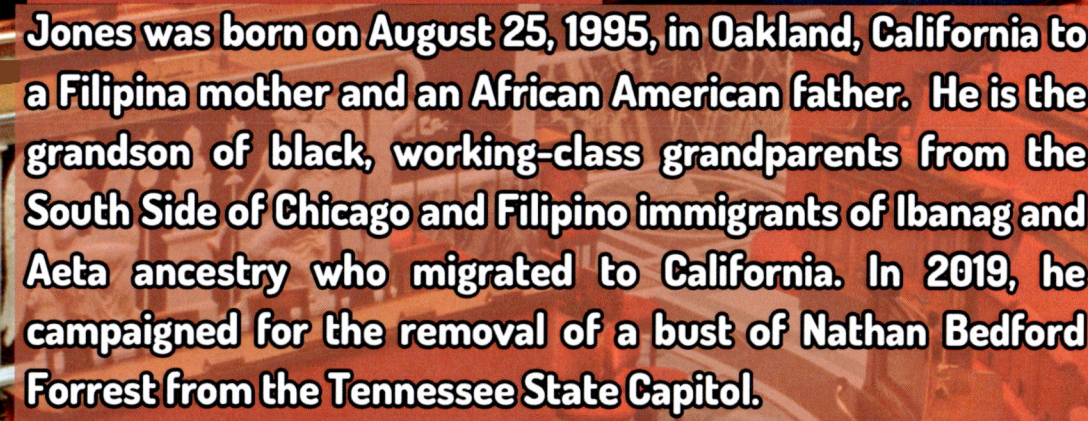

BIRTHPLACE: OAKLAND, CALIFORNIA - USA
BIRTH DATE: AUGUST 25, 1995
ETHNICITY: FILIPINO-AMERICAN
PROFESSION: ACTIVIST AND POLITICIAN FROM TENNESSEE

Jones was born on August 25, 1995, in Oakland, California to a Filipina mother and an African American father. He is the grandson of black, working-class grandparents from the South Side of Chicago and Filipino immigrants of Ibanag and Aeta ancestry who migrated to California. In 2019, he campaigned for the removal of a bust of Nathan Bedford Forrest from the Tennessee State Capitol.

In 2023 Jones joined a protest alongside Gloria Johnson and Justin J. Pearson for gun control reform that disrupted House proceedings at the state capitol. The Tennessee House voted on April 6, to expel Jones, alongside Pearson, who are both Black. Johnson, who is white, survived by one vote. Johnson argued that her race was the reason she was

not expelled, while Republican members noted that she did not take the protest as far as Jones and Pearson. Jones was appointed interim representative to his former seat by a unanimous vote of 36-0.

MAGDALENA CALLOWAY

BIRTHPLACE: PHILIPPINES
BIRTH DATE: JANUARY 1, 1911
DIED: APRIL 30,, 2000 (AGED 89) PARIS, FRANCE
ETHNICITY: FILIPINA-AMERICAN
PROFESSION: ACTRESS, VAUDEVILLE PERFORMER

Maggie Calloway was an actress born in the Philippines who rose to fame during the silent film and early sound film eras in the late 1920s and early 1930s. She was one of fourteen children born to John W. Calloway, an African-American former soldier in the United States Army, and his Filipina wife, Mamerta de la Rosa. A natural performer, her career began as a vaudeville actress in Manila, where she also starred in several silent films. She made her screen debut in Nepomeceno's 1928 film, Sampaguita, portraying a sampaguita vendor. In 1932, she appeared in two films- the silent film, Pugad ng Pag-ibig (Nest of Love) and the horror film, Ulong Inasnan (Salted-Head). In addition to her work in Manila, Calloway also performed with her husband's band in Penang, Malaysia, Singapore, and Shanghai. She later moved to the United States, where she continued to dance well into the 1970s. Maggie Calloway passed away on April 30, 2000, at the age of 89, and her death notice is listed under her married name, Magdalena Calloway Morgan.

In searching for Magdalena "Maggie" Calloway, there was not a lot of information about her available, especially because she became prominent so early in entertainment history, which is highly significant. Therefore, I am posting all of the information I found about her in this book.

Most of the information came from Singapore's publication, the Malaya Tribune.

The Malaya Tribune was the first English language daily newspaper founded in Singapore for an Asian readership. It began publication in Singapore on 1 January 1914 as an afternoon newspaper, and by the 1920s, it was distributed across Singapore, Malaya, Siam, Java, Sumatra and Borneo. The Malaya Tribune Press Limited expanded in the 1930s, creating a chain of newspapers that comprised the Sunday Tribune, the Morning Tribune, and their local editions for Kuala Lumpur, Ipoh and Penang. At the height of its circulation, Malaya Tribune was the largest daily newspaper in Malaya. However after suffering heavy losses during the Japanese Occupation and with rising post-war operating costs, the newspaper folded after publishing its last issue on 31 January 1951.

It appears she was well loved by the paper and it makes me wonder about how race was percieved in the Philippines during that era. Was being AfroFilipina more accepted during the early to mid 20th century?

SO LITTLE IS KNOWN ABOUT MAGGIE CALLOWAY SO FINDING THESE ARTICLES WAS LIKE FINDING GOLD.

The Silent Drama in the Philippines
By Al Elfrén Litiatco

Local interest in the silent drama which, after all, is but the reincarnation of the venerable art of pantomime, first manifested itself way back during the Spanish régime. At that time there was a form of amusement known as "Carillo." The carillos were forerunners of the modern photoplays and, like them, were largely though not wholly "silent."

A white sheet was placed across the opening of a window and looked just like the present screens in our cinematographs except that it was much smaller. Behind it, cardboard figures whose actions were verbally explained were manipulated like the puppets in a "Punch and Judy" show. A light was placed so as to throw the shadow of the marionettes on the screen.

It will be admitted that these primitive "movies" were very poor kind of entertainment. But then, our forefathers were not exacting — there was nothing better to be had in the way of pantomime — and the carillos attracted a fairly good number of people until motion pictures made their appearance.

THE FIRST "CINE"

It was in 1897 when the first "cine", located on or near the corner of Escolta and San Jacinto (now T. Pinpin), made its appearance. The admission price was one peso, an exorbitant charge for that period. But people will pay much to see something new in the way of entertainment, and the movies, then, were decided novelties. The pioneer "cine" flourished.

One peso entitled you to one session only. Today, fifty centavos will get you into, say, the Lyric, and, seated in a comfortable chair in a well-ventilated hall, you see a picture like "Resurrection," "Don Juan," "The Gaucho," "The Night of Love" or some film of the kind, as many times as it can be shown from 10:00 A. M. to 11:00 P. M., to especially adapted music played by a first-class orchestra, and without any danger of spoiling your eyesight.

Our fathers and grandfathers were not so fortunate. They had to pay one peso in an epoch when two and a half centavos could buy a good breakfast. They could see the entire show once only unless they were prepared to pay another peso. A session lasted about twenty minutes only. During that time about *twelve* "plays" were exhibited, and they didn't sooth the eyes either. They were entitled "A Train Collision," "The Cavalry," etc. and, as may be expected, they showed two trains colliding, several horsemen galloping by, and so on — a show less interesting than the news reels which so many now consider dull.

MAGGIE CALLOWAY, NATY FERNANDEZ, AND CONCEPCION FERNANDEZ IN "SAMPAGUITA"

But you should have seen the big parade that filed into that first cinematograph theater. You should have seen the people whose enthusiasm over *revistas* equalled our own over such screen masterpieces as "Seventh Heaven," "Don Q," and others of equal merit. You should have seen them cheerfully paying a peso for a place in a hall so crowded that the heat was almost suffocating. Well may we parody the title of the famous Fox film—What price movie!

Soon, however, "bigger and better pictures," as they put it nowadays, were served to an eager and liberal public.

THE NEW ERA

The era of better movies was inaugurated by a man called José Jimenez who, in 1903, opened a theater on Azcarraga street, in front of the railroad station. That "cine" was known as the "Cinematografo Rizal" and ran photoplays which, while better indeed than their predecessors, were not as good as the present two-reelers used merely as program fillers.

Naturally, the Cinematografo Rizal prospered. Cinemas sprang up everywhere: the Silent Drama had come to the Philippines, and to stay. It was firmly established in public favor.

The rest is commonly known. Today, all American pictures are shown here: Metro-Goldwyn-Meyer, Fox, Paramount, Universal, First National, United Artists, Warner Brothers, Film Booking Offices, Rayart, etc. Added to these we now import films from Germany, England, Italy, France, China, Japan, and other countries.

All of these films have evoked an encouraging response from the Philippine public. In fact, American producers have found such a profitable market here that a number of them are now—and more will be added to that number in the future, we doubt not—planning to erect their respective cinemas here showing their productions exclusively.

The Fox Film Corporation, for instance, will soon construct a modern theater and movie house, costing ₱300,000, on Carriedo street. It will be patterned after the Roxy Theatre in New York, will be provided with all the most up-to-date facilities, and will have a ₱13,000 organ forming a part of its orchestra.

Not to be outdone, the Universal Pictures Corporation plans to build *two* cinemas, of Spanish architecture, which will compare favorably with the Broadway movie palaces. Metro-Gold... already remodelled the Ideal, and talk Lyric is now current.

And all of these proposed expen... tified by the evident interest display

THE CITY OPERA.
Malaya Tribune, 28 September 1928, Page 7

THE CITY OPERA.
Philippine Company Still Strong Drawing Card.

On Wednesday night at the City Opera a new play entitled "The Nibelungs or the Dragon's Blood," with a most realistic dragon, was presented at the City Opera, and proved such a strong attraction that it is being repeated by special request tomorrow night. The play is full of thrills. Last night another of the popular all-vaudeville performances was given before an excellent audience, the Philippine Company being the strong attraction, though the best of Singapore's own artistes appeared in various Malay and Hindustani parts. The programme was an exceedingly varied one and one of the best we have ever seen at that popular place of amusement. Miss Maggie Calloway, the star of the aggregation, was as usual the life of the performance. A real "Rose of Erin," Miss Calloway possesses a fund of animal spirits and a perfection of health and physique which give her the exuberant vitality for which she is known here as well as on the China coast and in her

LATE SINGAPORE EDITION
The Singapore Free Press
AND DAILY NEWS

NO. 16,155.   ESTD. 1835   FRIDAY, AUGUST 2, 1940.   5 CENTS

TRY OUR Experienced TAILOR Miss YUN Who understands line and gives Character to your GOWNS... **CHOTIRMALL'S**

TOOTAL'S [crease resisting] **Striped Cotton** Suitable for Men's **PYJAMA SUITS**... In 12 different shades **CHOTIRMALL'S**

JAPAN PLANS "GREATER EAST ASIAN SPHERE"

Minister On Immediate Aim Of New Cabinet's Foreign Policy

SAYS N.I. & INDO-CHINA IN STABILITY REGION

Extremists Are Behind Tokio Arrests

OPPOSITION TO GOODWILL WORK

London, Aug. 1.

Sir Shenton On Malaya's £1 A Head For War

(From Our Own Correspondent)
London, Aug. 1.

BROADCASTING in the home service of the B.B.C. last night, the Governor of the Straits Settlements, Sir Shenton Thomas, paid a tribute to the patriotism of Malaya's population of 5,000,000, who had contributed to the Patriotic and War Funds and

INTENSIVE BOMBING BY R.A.F.

Italian Losses In Africa

SEA VIEW HOTEL TO-NIGHT
SPECIAL DINNER-DANCE & CABARET
DINNER $2.00   NON-DINERS $1.00
ENTERTAINMENT PROVIDED BY
MAGGIE CALLOWAY
TO-MORROW — EXTENSION TO 1 A.M.

"Buy a Bomber Ball" — War Fund — SEA VIEW HOTEL — AUGUST 31ST — MAKE THIS A DATE

Amusements
VICTORIA THEATRE
To-night, Last Night
AT 9.30 P.M.
Special Return Visit of The Chinese Operatic Gem of Shanghai
MISS MAY MAY LEE
and Her Talented Vaudeville Artistes.
SEE! The Film Stars in Real Life.
Stop!! Positively The Farewell Season at This Theatre.
Oh!!! Don't hesitate — Book your Seats early to avoid disappointment.

PLANS AND BOOKING NOW OPEN AT JOHN LITTLE'S.
POPULAR PRICES $1, $2, $3 AND $5

BEWARE! "THE GORILLA" IS COMING!

SPANISH TEA GARDENS
EAST COAST ROAD
OPEN AIR DANCING FLOOR

IMPRESSIONS OF SINGAPORE
What a Vaudeville Star Thinks Of Our City.

SORE, ACHING Swollen, Blistered Perspiring Tired Feet! **Zam-Buk GROWS NEW SKIN.**

(4) MORNING TRIBUNE, Wednesday, January 29, 1941.

Philippine Islands Folk Dance For Singapore Cabaret Show

THOSE who attend the Cabaret Dance which the Singapore Filipino Association will hold at the Cathay Cafe on February 9, will have the pleasure of seeing the first Singapore performance of "The Carinosa", a traditional Philippine folk dance.

"The Carinosa" is danced by five couples in Philippine country dress, which is most effective. The girls wear very full-sleeves blouses of fine gauzy material made from pineapple fibre, a "Tapis" of striped cotton and an underskirt of either cotton or organza.

The "Tapis" is a kind of sari of finely striped cotton material in gay colours. It is worn across the right shoulder and swathed round the waist and hips.

The complete costume is called

BY VERA

A "Balintawak" and one of the dancers who will take part in the show has one that she imported specially from Manila for the occasion. It has a blouse of pale green gauzy material embroidered with native motives, palm trees and blue sea. Bits of...

"The Carinosa" begins with the couples forming two lines and going through the actions of planting rice, while they sing a folk song with native words.

Then they invite others to join them, chanting words which mean "You come with us" and making a "hitch hikers" gesture with one thumb.

A country dance, with much coquetting by the girls and coy hiding of their faces, follows. Finally they accept their partner's invitations to waltz. The dance ends with a line-up of the performers who go off to the strains of a lively tune in march time.

Other cabaret attractions include an exhibition of America's latest dance craze "The Conga," which swept the country after its appearance in the New York stage hit

ARDMORE

"Too many girls." Rose and Conrad will dance this variation of the rhumba. Rose wears a red rhumba costume with a frilled skirt and

Martin, Santos, Cruz and Borlongan.

Mrs. Bond is convalescing after a serious illness and the change of air should hasten her complete recovery.

* * *

A large number of Singaporeans enjoyed the hospitality of their Chinese friends on Monday and several large parties were held to celebrate the New Year.

Dato and Datin S. Q. Wong, who have held a morning pahit party on this occasion for the past five years, were "At home" to their many friends, and visitors included:— Sir Percy and Lady Mc-Elwaine, Lady Bagnall, Comte and Comtesse de Coursulles, Mr. and Mrs. Kenneth S. Patton, Mr. and Mrs. H. G. Minnigerode, Mr. and Mrs. Harold Robison, Mr. and Mrs. F. C. Edwards, Mr. and Mrs. F. W. Hall, Miss Dorothy Owen, Mrs. Hilterman and Miss Nicoll-Jones.

Mrs. Lee Choon Guan, M.B.E. and Mr. and Mrs. Lee Chim Tuan, whose New Year parties have become quite a tradition, held another delightful one on Monday. Among the guests were:— Mr. and Mrs. Tay Lian Teck, Mr. Justice A'Beckett Terrell and family, Mr. and Mrs. P. W.

People and Places

Preparing For Feb. 9 Floor Show

Miss Maggie Calloway, who is training the dancers who will take part in cabaret items at the Cabaret Tea Dance to be given by the Singapore Filipino Association at the Cathay Cafe, on Feb. 9. Miss Calloway was educated in the U.S.A. and spent dancing

London at the moment, according to Mr. Henry Kavanaugh of Fridge's hairdressing department, is a straight bob with curly ends, the hair being swept back leaving from the forehead in Grecian curls and heavy waves are quite out.

To combat winter gloom many colours have come into their own

PUBLIC AMUSEMENTS.

Successful Vaudeville Night.

The City Opera Company, consisting of Malay and Filipino artists, presented a very successful vaudeville programme before a large and appreciable house at the Moonlight Hall (New World Shows) last night. The bill was varied, and was one which catered for a cosmopolitan audience.

Maggie Calloway was in great demand. Indeed, the audience were cruel in their calls for encores. **Maggie** pleased immensely in "The Roof Blues," charlestoning and singing on top of the piano with that ease and abandon only expected of an accomplished artist.

Henry was as eccentric and as humorous as ever, and Eddie, with his clear tenor voice, shared largely in the success.

Marina, Olga and Didang must not be forgotten, nor should Menah, the "star" among the Malay artists, who, together with Henry, had to respond to six encores.

The orchestra, under the able baton of Mr. Martinez, rendered very appreciable selections.

IMPRESSIONS OF SINGAPORE.

What a Vaudeville Star Thinks Of Our City.

Miss **Maggie Calloway**, the brilliant star of the City Opera, imported from the Philippine Islands, writes to the "Philippines Herald" her opinions of Singapore which prove very flattering to our local pride. She says:

"Contrary to my expectations be-

THE AFROFILIPINO RENAISSANCE

Renaissance means rebirth and this generation has taken their roots to a new level, giving birth to a bolder sense of pride. It is truly inspiring to witness the younger generation express and celebrate their Filipino heritage confidently, without reservation. They drape themselves in the Filipino flag, some have acquired citizenship and others make sure people acknowledge them and do not invisibilize any part of their being, which is a beautiful thing to behold.

Here are just a few Afrofilipinos - boldly and unapolegetically declaring their roots. They make me so, so, proud.

AFROFILIPINA MAGANDA

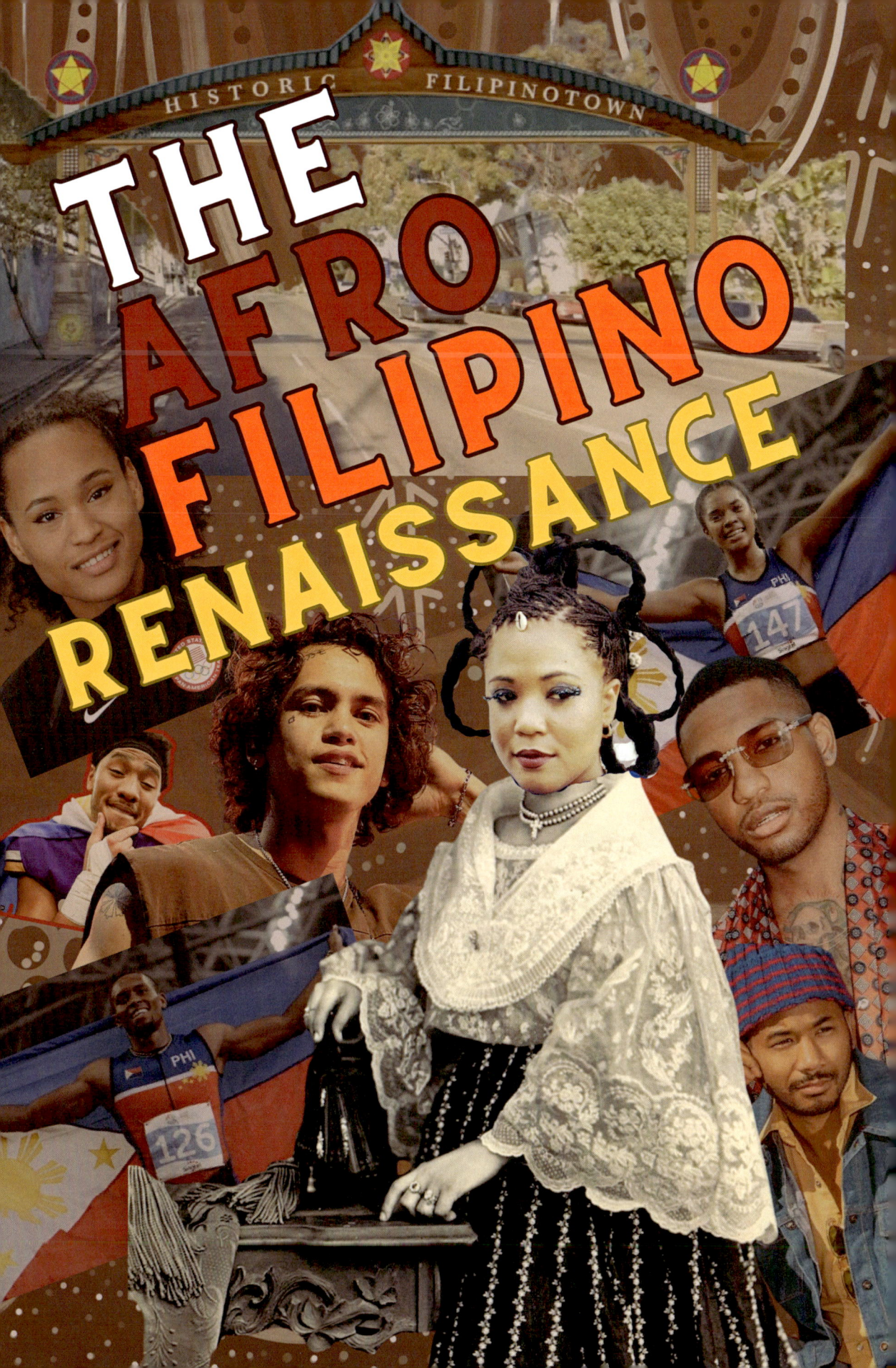

KAYLA RICHARDSON
SOUTH EAST ASIA GAMES GOLD MEDALIST – 100 M

Being proud of my Filipino heritage is something that has continued to develop as I've grown up and gone through different experiences. My grandparents Felixberto and Ludivina Maico immigrated to the United States from the Philippines with their 3 children, despite their love for the life they had in Zamboanga, in order to give their family a better life with greater opportunities. Spending a lot of my childhood with my grandparents I've heard many stories about their life in the Philippines and how our family started. Even after hearing all the stories and learning about the Filipino culture, I was still unsure about what it all meant. When I was a little girl, my 3 sisters and I would go everywhere with my grandparents and we would all get stared at often. Being half Filipino and half Black, I knew we looked different from my grandparents, but I wasn't able to fully understand. It was something that we just recognized and laughed off, but it still made me uncomfortable with who I was in certain settings. As a mixed race individual, I never felt like I completely fit in with either side of my heritage. It wasn't until I got to high school that I was able to fully embrace and appreciate my biracial heritage and be proud and comfortable with who I was.

excerpt from "In Their Own Words"
UCIrvinesports.com

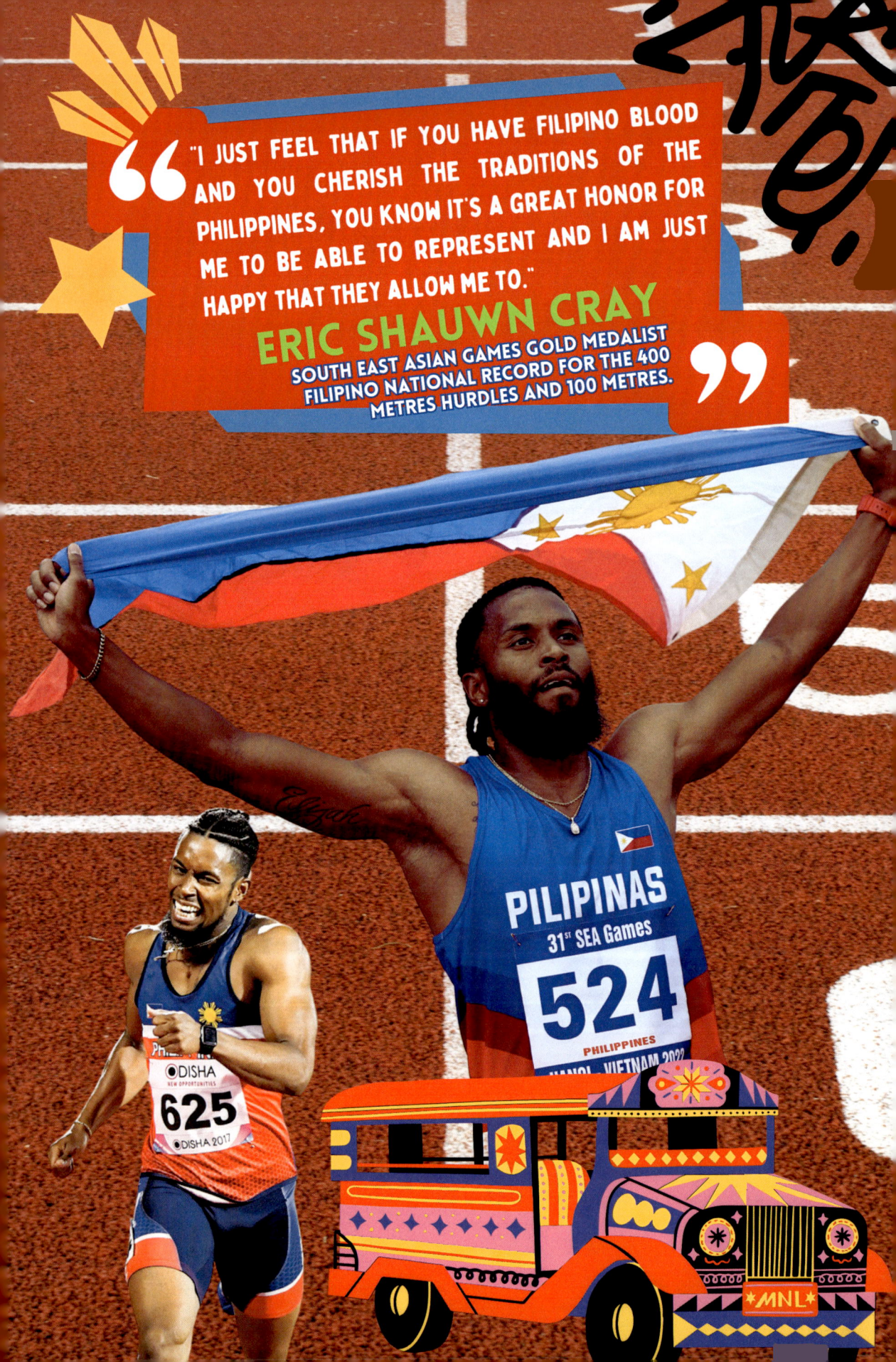

> "I think the one thing that really attracts me to taekwondo is the diversity of all...There's so many different backgrounds of people and it's never a specific type of person that always wins — it's anybody's day, anybody's game, anybody's time to become champion."
>
> **PAIGE MCPHERSON**
> OLYMPIC TAE KWAN DO COMPETITOR
>
> SOURCE: NBC NEWS

> "I'M FLAMBOYANT WITH MY TASTE IN FASHION...SO, YOU HAVE THIS HANDSOME, FLASHY BLACK CHILD WALKING AROUND WITH THIS SUPER MODEST, HUMBLE FILIPINO LADY, AND SOME WOULD BE LIKE, 'WHAT'S GOING ON?' I ALSO EXPERIENCED SOME PREJUDICE FROM OLDER FILIPINOS, WHO WOULD CRACK JOKES ABOUT MY DARK SKIN. THAT HURT MY FEELINGS, TOO. SO I HAD TO DODGE BULLETS FROM BOTH SIDES."
>
> **GUAPDAD**
> RAPPER, CREATIVE, FASHIONISTA

> **ON PROMOTING HIS MAHAL ALBUM USING A JEEPNEY**
>
> The fact that this American thing had gone to the Philippines, and got reappropriated to be this Filipino art piece. And now it's back in the States where there is another level of life to it.
>
> **CHAZ BEAR**
> TORO Y MOI - SINGER, SONGWRITER, RECORD PRODUCER, AND GRAPHIC DESIGNER.

PHOTO: CHRIS MAGGIO.   SOURCE: GQ MAGAZINE

THERE ARE SO MANY MORE RENAISSANCE AFROFILIPINOS

FROM ACTIVISTS TO SOCIAL MEDIA INFLUENCERS, ACTORS TO EDUCATORS, FARMERS TO POLITICIANS, AFRO-FILIPINOS TAKE PRIDE IN THEIR HERITAGE, AND IT'S BEEN A LONG TIME COMING.

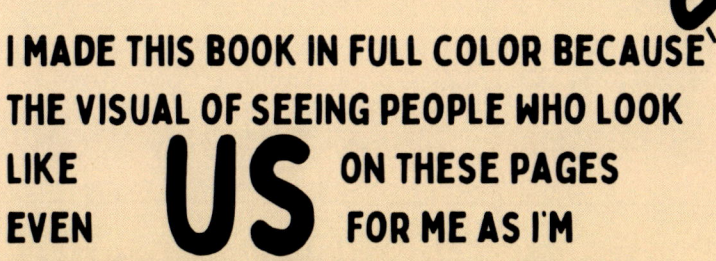

I MADE THIS BOOK IN FULL COLOR BECAUSE THE VISUAL OF SEEING PEOPLE WHO LOOK LIKE **US** ON THESE PAGES EVEN FOR ME AS I'M WRITING THIS MAKES ME FEEL SOOOOO... **SEEN**

AND WE CANNOT STOP. MY HOPE IS THAT OTHERS WILL CONTINUE WRITING OUR HISTORY IN OUR VOICE AND CONTINUE TO CREATE MATERIALS THAT SHOW OUR BEAUTIFUL AFROFILIPINO HISTORY & CULTURE.

BEYOND THE STORM

We are the resilient souls who have endured the storm. Hopefully, future generations will have increased visibility and representation, and we won't need any more "firsts." Even though this IS the FIRST AfroFilipino History Book EVER, I am confident it will not be the last. The aim of this endeavour is not to highlight any singularity or individuality, but rather to pave the way for upcoming generations, ensuring a clearer path for all. None of us can get there alone, there is room for us ALL – there is need for us ALL!

This is my homage to YOU, actually to US. Our narrative is no longer silenced or erased. This is monumental. Our initial history is penned by an AfroFilipina, filled with immense love and respect for ALL that we encompass. Let us continue to protect the volcano that is life.

OMILANI ALARCON - FOUNDER AFROFILIPINA

MAGANDANG ITIM

I remember when they told me
I didn't belong
That was way before
I had this song
Magandang Morena - you're beautiful

You're beautiful
Magandang Morena - Magandang itim

Itim means BLACK in Tagalog
I ain't trying to ruffle no feathers,
I'm just trying to start some dialogue
See why should I be treated in disdain
Like I'm a stain I'm trying to refrain
From this poison in my brain

Didn't you know
Insulting me ain't gonna give you no hope
Entitled ones feel enlightened like Papaya Soap
I carry the blood of the Mansaka and the Mandaya
I am the Mindanao child returned
And I walk through the fire

Morena and proud
Beautiful ITIM
It's just an ordinary day in the life of this QUEEN
It's just an ordinary day in the life of this queen
It's just an ordinary day
Never forget who you are, ha-ha

MAGANDANG ITIM

Morena and proud
Beautiful ITIM
It's just an ordinary day in the life of this QUEEN
It's just an ordinary day in the life of this queen
It's just an ordinary day
Never forget who you are, ha-ha

Magandang Morena
MAGANDANG ITIM

This is for those who've been told
You'd be pretty if you weren't so dark
This is for the AfroPinays and Pinoys
Who've been told you don't look Filipino at ALL
Those who get those unwelcoming stares
When they walk through the door
It used to hurt me so bad
But I can't even feel it no more

Magandang Morena
Don't let nobody take your sunshine away
MAGANDANG ITIM
We are beautiful and melanated
Divinely created
AfroPinay we so fly it's amazing
AROPINAY WE SO FLY IT'S AMAZING
AFROPINAY WE SO FLY IT'S AMAZING
AfroPinay we so fly!

BIBLIOGRAPHY

Angeles, S. (2023). NFL's Josh Jacobs on representing Filipino pride. ABS-CBN News. https://news.abs-cbn.com/sports/02/13/23/nfls-josh-jacobs-on-representing-filipino-pride.

Black Filipino Artist Reveals Discrimination Growing up in Oakland. (2021, April 15). Yahoo News. https://news.yahoo.com/black-filipino-artist-reveals-discrimination-211339900.html

Cook Cole, Mabel. (1916). Philippine Folk Tales. Chicago: A.C. McClurg & Co., 187.

For Olympian Paige McPherson, taekwondo is a "home away from home." (2017, June 6). NBC News. https://www.nbcnews.com/news/asian-america/olympic-taekwondo-fighter-paige-mcpherson-sets-sights-world-championship-n763971

In Their Own Words: Kayla Richardson. (n.d.). UCI Athletics. Retrieved January 31, 2024, from https://ucirvinesports.com/news/2021/5/24/features-in-their-own-words-kayla-richardson.aspx

Iyer, P. (2020a, December 22). Filipino basketball's forgotten Trailblazer: The eternal legacy of Raymond Townsend. AMAZN HQ. https://amaznhq.com/filipino-basketballs-forgotten-trailblazer-the-eternal-legacy-of-raymond-townsend/

Kendi, D. I. X. (2016). Stamped from the beginning. Avalon Publishing Group.

Layugan, Owen. personal communication, January 4, 2024

Litiatco, A. E. (1928). The Silent Drama in the Philippines. Philippine Education Magazine, 25, 117. https://doi.org/1/17/2024

BIBLIOGRAPHY

#MAGANDANGMORENX: Beautiful brown skin. ASIA JACKSON. (2016). https://www.asiajackson.com/magandang-morenx

Malaya Tribune - (1928). THE CITY OPERA Philippine Company Still Strong Drawing Card. 7. https://doi.org/1/17/2024

Melchor, A. (2023, March 8). Indigenous Filipino group has highest known Denisovan ancestry. The Scientist Magazine®. https://www.the-scientist.com/news-opinion/indigenous-filipino-group-has-highest-known-denisovan-ancestry-69089

Nast, C. (2022, July 8). Toro y Moi on Embracing His Filipino Culture With His New Album and Working With Eric Andre. GQ. https://www.gq.com/story/toro-y-moi-mahal-eric-andre-jeepney-interview

Orejas, T. (2023, January 25). First Aeta to pass criminology board exam to fulfill dream of becoming a cop. INQUIRER.net. https://newsinfo.inquirer.net/1720582/first-aeta-to-pass-criminology-board-exam-to-fulfill-dream-of-becoming-a-cop

Philippines, L. (n.d.). Lalahon. Visayan Mythologies of the Philippines. http://vizayanmyths.blogspot.com/2013/05/normal-0-false-false-false.html

R. J. Terry, ROBERT BENNETT BEAN, 1874–1944, American Anthropologist, 10.1525/aa.1946.48.1.02a00080, 48, 1, (70-74), (2009).

Students, R. B. and U. A. 360 2019. (2020). T'Nalak: The Land of the Dreamweavers. Uw.pressbooks.pub. https://uw.pressbooks.pub/criticalfilipinxamericanhistories/chapter/tnalak-the-land-of-the-dreamweavers/#:~:text=T%27nalak%20is%20a%20traditional

WE ARE BEAUTIFUL

WE ARE NOT ALONE

BLACK IS BEAUTIFUL

MAGANDANG ITIM

YOU ARE FILIPINO ENOUGH

YOU ARE BLACK ENOUGH

YOU ARE HUMAN ENOUGH

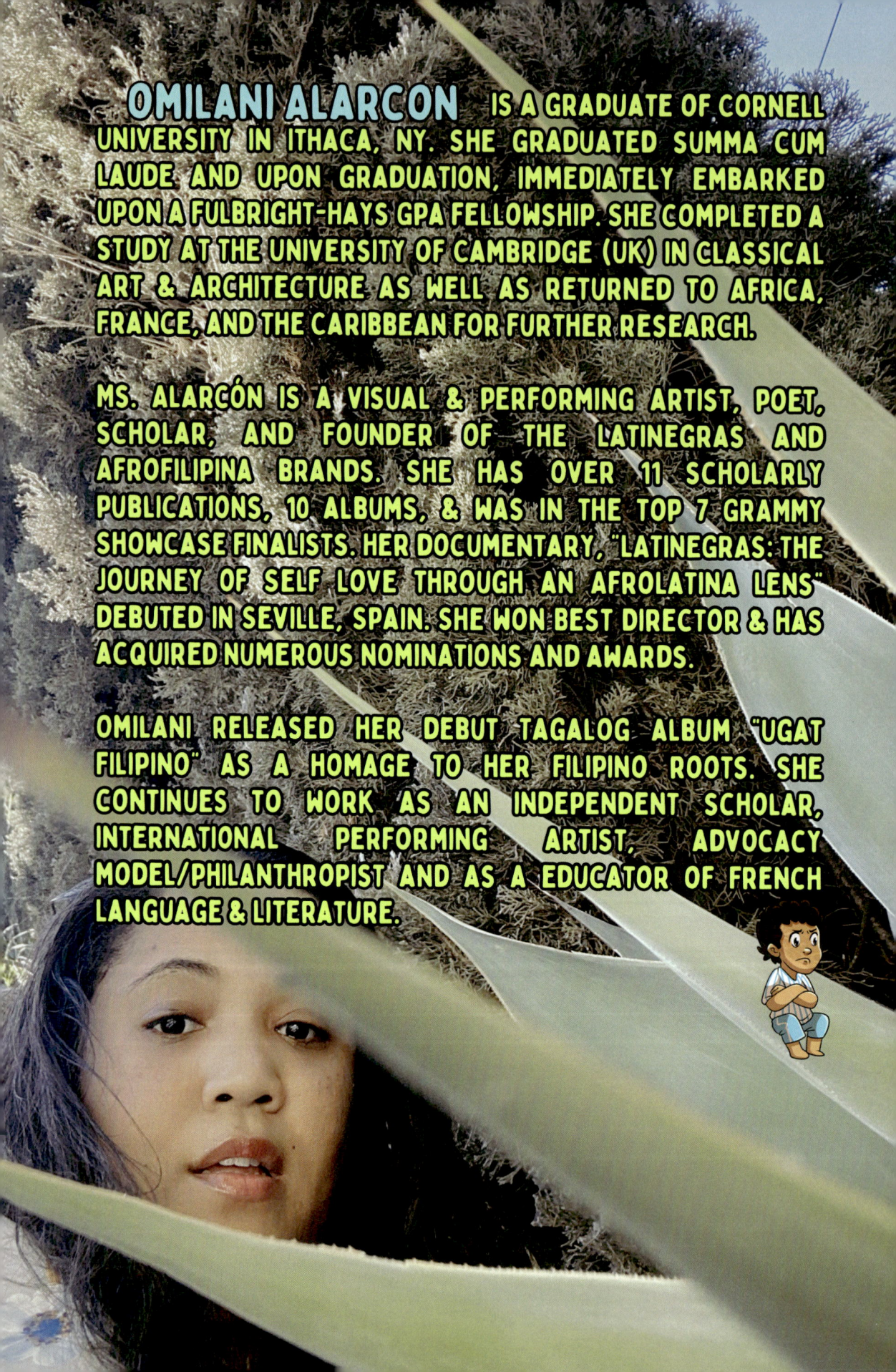

OMILANI ALARCON is a graduate of Cornell University in Ithaca, NY. She graduated summa cum laude and upon graduation, immediately embarked upon a Fulbright-Hays GPA fellowship. She completed a study at the University of Cambridge (UK) in classical art & architecture as well as returned to Africa, France, and the Caribbean for further research.

Ms. Alarcón is a visual & performing artist, poet, scholar, and founder of the Latinegras and Afrofilipina brands. She has over 11 scholarly publications, 10 albums, & was in the top 7 Grammy showcase finalists. Her documentary, "Latinegras: The Journey of Self Love Through An Afrolatina Lens" debuted in Seville, Spain. She won Best Director & has acquired numerous nominations and awards.

Omilani released her debut Tagalog album "Ugat Filipino" as a homage to her Filipino roots. She continues to work as an independent scholar, international performing artist, advocacy model/philanthropist and as a educator of French language & literature.